CapCut

For Creators

The Ultimate Guide

to Stunning Video Editing

O. Owais

TABLE OF CONTENTS

INTRODUCTION

More powerful than ever, video content is revolutionizing how we inspire, connect, and share. Making engaging videos can help you stand out in a crowded digital market, whether you're a social media influencer, content provider, or aspiring filmmaker. CapCut, a feature-rich yet user-friendly video editing application, becomes the ideal creative partner in this situation.

This book will teach you everything you need to know to edit videos confidently and stylishly, taking you from novice to expert. There are useful suggestions and actionable insights to help you realize your vision, whether you're making your first vlog, a lesson, or a cinematic masterpiece.

You'll learn the fundamentals of video editing while also delving into more complex methods like visual effects, audio polishing, and imaginative narrative thanks to concise explanations, detailed directions, and captivating examples. Additionally, you will learn how to turn your ideas into engaging content by taking on real-world projects like fitness demonstrations, vacation trips, and more.

The technical issues are not the only focus of this book, though. Additionally, it's about pushing the envelope of what's feasible and letting your creativity run wild. This resource, when combined with extra video tutorials and motivational images, will enable you to create videos that are not just well-executed but also profoundly powerful.

Are you prepared to make your dream a reality? Together, let's set off on this creative adventure. Your tale is just waiting to be told using CapCut, and the possibilities are unlimited.

WHO IS THIS BOOK FOR?

This book is for anyone who wants to step up their video-editing game and create content that truly stands out. Whether you're a beginner testing the waters or a seasoned creator looking to refine your skills, you'll find practical tips, techniques, and inspiration here.

Are you a **content creator** on platforms like YouTube, TikTok, or Instagram? This book will help you produce professional-quality videos that grab attention and keep your audience engaged.

Perhaps you're an influencer on social media looking to elevate your brand. Learn how to create polished, visually appealing content that boosts your presence and connects with your followers.

If you're an **aspiring filmmaker** or storyteller, this guide will help you translate your ideas into stunning visuals that capture emotion and creativity.

For **vloggers, educators, or coaches**, this book provides the tools to make your videos not just informative, but truly memorable.

Even if you're a **business owner** or **marketer** looking to use video to promote your products or services, you'll discover how to make content that's both professional and persuasive. No matter who you are, if you want to create videos that look and feel amazing—without needing years of experience—this book is for you. Let's get started!

CHAPTER 1

A QUICK OVERVIEW OF CAPCUT

CapCut is a free and easy-to-use video editing tool that lets users quickly create high-quality videos from their smartphones. CapCut is made to accommodate users of all skill levels with its array of user-friendly features, which include cutting, speed changes, reversals, music integration, stickers, and text. It is a flexible tool for video editing on multiple platforms because it works with Windows, mobile devices, and web platforms. CapCut guarantees that your videos have a polished, expert appearance whether you're editing them for YouTube, Facebook, Instagram, or TikTok.

All skill levels can use CapCut thanks to its many user-friendly features, which include cutting, speed changes, reversals, music integration, stickers, and writing. Due to its compatibility with Windows, mobile devices, and web platforms, it is a multiplatform video editing application. Regardless of whether you're editing for YouTube, Facebook, Instagram, or TikTok, CapCut guarantees that your videos will seem clean and expert.

Many vendors are using CapCut to edit their advertising movies as TikTok Shops expand internationally. Sellers highlight their top-selling items with CapCut's well-liked, hilarious templates, producing eye-catching material that receives millions of views. CapCut makes it simple to produce engaging material that stands out on TikTok Shop, from product demos to visually appealing listings.

CapCut is useful for user-generated content producers as well, who use it to create distinctive, memorable advertisements for companies. One-of-a-kind material allows artists to keep a competitive edge and earn premium pricing.

CapCut's growing popularity is evident, as it has surpassed 200 million Monthly Active Users. This milestone has solidified CapCut's position as ByteDance's second overseas-focused product to reach over 100 million Monthly Active Users, showcasing its global appeal and widespread adoption.

What you will learn:

- CapCut overview
- The latest features in CapCut
- The latest features in CapCut
- CapCut interface - desktop
- Device compatibility and system requirements
- How to get CapCut and install it
- Maximize the value of this book
- How to use CapCut like a pro

LATEST FEATURES IN CAPCUT

1. **AI-Powered Tools**: AI-powered capabilities that help with automatic scene detection, backdrop removal, and intelligent video cropping is frequently included in CapCut.

2. **Enhanced Editing Tools**: Advanced cutting choices, speed changes, and frame-by-frame editing capabilities are among the new tools for accurate editing.

3. **Templates and Effects**: an expanding collection of pre-made effects and themes that let users quickly produce videos with a polished appearance.

6

4. **Text and Title Customization**: enhanced text capabilities for creating titles and captions for films that provide additional fonts, animations, and styles.
5. **Audio Features**: Improved audio editing features, such as sound effects, voiceover choices with better controls, and background music integration.
6. **Multi-Track Editing**: Multi-track editing is supported, enabling users to combine several audio and video tracks for more intricate projects.
7. **Collaboration Features**: Tools that make it simpler for people to collaborate, making it possible to share and co-edit projects.
8. **Export Options**: expanded export options that enable outputs with higher resolution and a range of file formats appropriate for various platforms (e.g., social media).
9. **User Interface Improvements**: A more user-friendly interface with easier navigation and easier access to tools to improve the user experience.

CAPCUT PLATFORMS & EDITORS

CapCut makes editing photos and videos simple, wherever you are. Whether you're using a desktop computer, tablet, or smartphone, CapCut's platforms and editors are made to enable you to produce content that looks professional without requiring a lot of experience. You can rapidly edit films, add effects, or customize photos for social media, business, or personal use with its easy-to-use interface and clever features like AI-powered tools. Additionally, CapCut provides cloud storage for smooth cross-device editing and sharing. CapCut includes everything you need to realize your imaginative ideas, whether your goal is a fast edit or a finished, high-quality project.

Mobile Video Editor for Free:
- Simplify the production of videos for business or personal branding.
- Make use of clever features such as multi-language video transcription, text-to-speech, and speech-to-text.
- With only one click, you can quickly eliminate video backgrounds.
- Add sound effects, text overlays, and current music to videos to make them better.
- CapCut offers cloud storage for smooth media sharing and management.

Free Photo Editor for Mobile Devices

- CapCut's AI-powered photo editor allows you to create and modify images for free.
- Savor background removal, resizing, and color matching.
- Importing pictures from your smartphone or online storage is simple.
- Check out the text overlays, filters, effects, and templates.
- Make changes to the file details before posting it on social media.

Free Video Editor for Desktops

- The desktop video editor from CapCut combines expertise and AI capability.
- Your job is streamlined with features like Auto Reframe, Auto Captions, and Script to Video.
- Shortcuts that increase productivity are part of the user-friendly interface.
- Get access to thousands of free effects, animations, transitions, keyframe animations, extensive text options, and multilingual AI-generated captions.

- For exceptional quality, export in breathtaking 4K 60fps, enabling users of all skill levels to create anywhere.

CAPCUT INTERFACE - DESKTOP

The user-friendly interface of CapCut makes it simple for both novice and seasoned editors to produce stunning videos. The interface is notable for the following reasons:

- ✓ **Intuitive Layout**: The clean and organized design allows for easy navigation, ensuring users can quickly access all the tools they need.
- ✓ **Drag-and-Drop Functionality**: With its drag-and-drop interface, users can effortlessly add and arrange media clips in the timeline.

- ✓ **Timeline View**: The timeline is simple to use, providing a clear view of your project and allowing for precise editing.
- ✓ **Preview Window**: The real-time preview window allows users to instantly view their edits, making it easier to tweak and refine footage.
- ✓ **Easy Access to Tools**: All essential tools—cutting, trimming, transitions, and effects—are readily accessible, minimizing the time spent searching for features.
- ✓ **Multi-Layer Editing**: CapCut supports multi-layer editing, enabling users to work with multiple video, audio, and image tracks simultaneously.
- ✓ **Customization Options**: It provides a variety of customization options, from visual effects to text overlays, allowing you to tailor your content to your exact needs.
- ✓ **Real-Time Syncing**: Edits are automatically synced, which means you can work seamlessly without worrying about losing progress.
- ✓ **Cross-Platform Compatibility**: CapCut offers cloud storage and synchronization, making it easy to work across multiple devices.

Comprehensive Editing Tools:

CapCut provides a vast range of all-inclusive editing tools to assist content producers in producing polished and captivating videos. Here is a summary of its main attributes:

Basic Editing Tools

- **Cutting**: Videos can be easily divided into smaller parts to eliminate unnecessary scenes.
- **Trimming**: Trim the beginning or conclusion of your footage to make it perfect.
- **Splitting Videos**: To effectively organize your content, divide lengthy clips into manageable chunks.
- **Adjusting Speed**: You can adjust the speed of your clips to make them go more slowly or more quickly.
- **Merging Clips**: Easily merge several segments into a single, coherent video.

Advanced Effects and Transitions

CapCut elevates your video editing with its array of advanced visual effects and transitions that give your material a polished look.

- **Cinematic Filters**: Use filters to give your video a professional, cinematic appearance.
- **Color Grading**: For a more polished and cinematic look, change the color palette and tones.
- **Special Effects**: To add uniqueness to your films, use a range of effects.
- **Dramatic Transitions**: To keep the flow engaging, provide seamless and striking transitions between clips.
- **Slow-Motion Effects**: To add dramatic impact, slow down certain portions of your video.
- **Motion Tracking**: To create dynamic effects in your video, track and work with moving objects.
- **Glitch Effects**: Use glitch effects to create a digital or futuristic look.
- **Vintage Effects**: Use nostalgic vintage styles and filters to create a retro vibe.
- **Light Leaks**: For a dreamier, more creative feel, add subtle lighting effects.
- **Vignette Effects**: To draw emphasis to the center of the frame and darken the corners, include a vignette.

With these potent features, CapCut helps you create visually stunning and intriguing material that tells captivating stories to your audience.

DEVICE COMPATIBILITY AND SYSTEM REQUIREMENTS

Device Compatibility:

Make sure your device is up to current, including smartphones running the most recent iterations of iOS or Android. If you're a desktop user, make sure your computer satisfies the requirements for the desktop version of CapCut.

CapCut Desktop System Requirements
Operating System:

macOS 10.15 (Catalina) or later

Windows 10 or later

Processor:

Minimum: Intel Core i3 or equivalent

Recommended: For improved performance, use an Intel Core i5 or higher.

RAM:

Minimum: 4 GB

Recommended: For best results, use 8 GB or more, especially when working on bigger projects.

Graphics Card:

Integrated graphics for simple editing jobs.

Recommended: A specialized GPU (AMD or NVIDIA) for more complex editing and quicker rendering.

Storage:

Minimum 2 GB of free disk space for installation

Additional storage is required for media files and project files

Display:

Minimum resolution: 1280x720 pixels

Recommended resolution: 1920x1080 pixels or higher for the best visual experience

Internet Connection:

Required for downloading the software, accessing online resources, and exporting directly to social media platforms.

Additional Software:

Ensure drivers are up-to-date for various hardware components, including your graphics card.

To guarantee a smooth and efficient editing experience with CapCut on your desktop, make sure your system meets or exceeds these requirements.

HOW TO GET CAPCUT AND INSTALL IT

CapCut for Desktop Installation

CapCut is available for PC and Mac as a free desktop software, as well as an online editing tool. Here's how to download and install CapCut on your desktop:

- **Download Process**:
  1. Open your search engine and visit the official CapCut Desktop page:

     https://www.CapCut.com/tools/desktop-video-editor

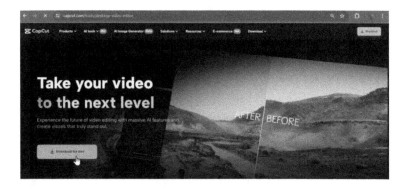

  1. On the page, click the "Download" button.
  2. If redirected, wait for the **download** file to download automatically.

3. Click the file to begin the installation process after it has finished downloading, then follow the instructions to set up CapCut on your desktop.

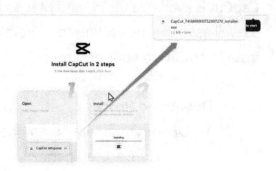

CapCut for Mobile (iOS and Android):

CapCut is also available for both iOS and Android devices, offering a streamlined mobile editing experience.

- **Download Process**:

    1. **iOS Users**: Go to the **App Store**, search for **CapCut**, and click **Get** to install the app.

17

2. **Android Users**: Visit the **Google Play Store**, search for **CapCut**, and tap **Install** to download the app.

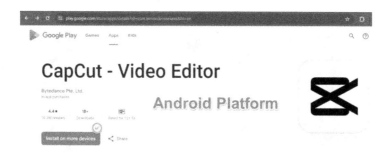

CapCut for mobile is free to use and provides a wide range of features, making it easy to edit and share videos directly from your device.

General Tips for Installing CapCut

- Ensure your device has a stable internet connection before downloading the app to avoid interruptions during the download process.
- After installation, open the app or desktop software and begin editing your videos with the easy-to-use tools CapCut provides.

Guide for Windows Installation:

While you are still connected to the internet, simply click the Downloaded installer to begin the installation.

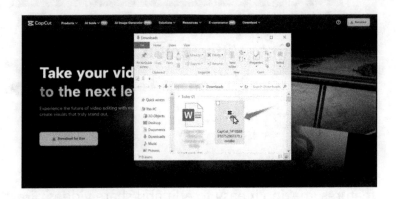

Once you've double-clicked or opened the CapCut file as an admin from your download folder, quickly respond to the on-screen prompt by accepting Yes to continue.

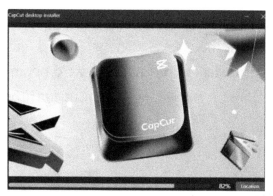

Await the progress; depending on your internet speed, it shouldn't take long. After installation, launch CapCut from the desktop's "Start" menu. You may be prompted to sign in with your Google, Facebook, or TikTok account to use the program, but it's not required.

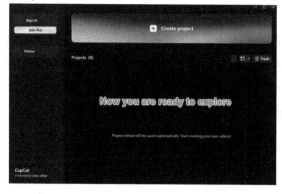

It is very fantastic that you are now prepared to embark on your journey!

If you prefer not to install a lot of apps because you can find them online, the CapCut Online Editing Platform is available to you; no installation is necessary. To begin, quickly click the linked link: https://www.CapCut.com/tools/online-video-editor

When the page loads completely, click to open, and if necessary, create an account with Google or another service. You can start the tour as soon as your data are verified. The user interface looks like this. You can now import or upload your media components and begin editing.

Notice: Regardless of whether you are using the desktop, mobile, or online Desktop edition, it is assumed that you will construct your projects with your data-enabled during the sessions.

CapCut: Desktop vs. Mobile

CapCut is a popular video editing application available for both desktop and mobile devices. Each version caters to different needs, offering unique advantages:

- **Mobile Version**: Designed for on-the-go editing, the mobile app provides an intuitive interface and the convenience of editing directly from your smartphone. Its simplicity makes it ideal for quick edits and casual users.

22

- **Desktop Version**: The desktop version offers a more robust editing experience, leveraging the larger screen and greater processing power of a computer. This allows for advanced editing techniques, precise adjustments, and the ability to manage complex projects with ease.

Whether you prefer the flexibility of mobile editing or the extensive capabilities of the desktop version, CapCut ensures a seamless video editing experience tailored to your needs.

MAXIMIZE THE VALUE OF THIS BOOK

This book is more than a guide—it's your toolkit for achieving success and unlocking new skills. To fully benefit from its insights, approach it with intention and determination. Here's how to maximize it:

- **Engage with Purpose**: Maintain your curiosity and be prepared to try new things as you approach each segment with an open mind and a dedication to implementing ideas.

- **Practice Consistently**: Apply the methods and strategies described consistently to turn knowledge into skill. Repetition boosts confidence and solidifies information.

- **Experiment Fearlessly**: Trying something new leads to innovation. Don't be afraid to try out the suggested tools, approaches, and tactics. Find out what suits you the most.

- **Reflect on Progress**: Take a moment to assess your progress after completing a chapter or task. Thinking back on what you've studied helps you find areas for development and solidify your knowledge.

- **Apply to Real-World Projects**: Apply your newly acquired abilities to your personal or professional endeavors. The instant application produces useful outcomes and helps solidify information.

- **Seek Constructive Feedback**: Present your work to others or contrast it with the book's examples. Peer or mentor constructive criticism can help you improve your skills and provide insightful information. Meet other creators here, CapCut Creative Space: https://discord.com/channels/

- **Stay Adaptable:** Not every strategy or technique will work for you. For optimal results, adjust the book's recommendations to fit your objectives and particular style.

- **Revisit and Reinforce**: Learning is a continuous process. To keep on course and gain a deeper comprehension, go back to important parts of the text as needed.

Approach this book with curiosity, diligence, and a willingness to grow. By actively engaging, experimenting, and applying the lessons, you'll transform knowledge into tangible success and realize your full potential!

HOW TO USE CAPCUT LIKE A PRO

Creating stunning videos with CapCut is simple and efficient if you follow these steps.

1. Plan Your Project

- **Define Your Purpose**: Think about the goal of your video. Is it a tutorial, a vlog, or a promotional clip? Knowing this will shape your approach.

- **Storyboard Your Idea**: Sketch out the sequence of scenes to visualize how your video will flow.

- **Gather Your Media**: Collect all the video clips, images, music, and other materials you'll need in one place.

2. Stay Organized

- **Create a Project Folder**: Make a dedicated folder on your computer to keep everything neatly stored.

- **Name Your Files Clearly**: Use descriptive names for easy identification when importing them into CapCut.

3. Start Editing in CapCut

- **Launch the App**: Open CapCut on your Mobile device or desktop.

- **Import Your Media**: Bring in your files from your project folder or directly from cloud services like Dropbox or Google Drive.

- **Arrange Your Clips**: Drag and drop media onto the timeline, organizing it according to your storyboard plan.

4. Edit Your Video Like a Pro

- **Trim and Tweak**: Use CapCut's tools to cut unwanted sections, add smooth transitions, and apply filters for a polished look.

- **Adjust and Enhance**: Refine colors, brightness, and contrast. To draw attention to crucial information or to give context, use text overlays.

5. Add the Special Touches

- **Use Templates and Presets**: Choose from CapCut's pre-designed templates for a professional finish without starting from scratch.

- **Animate with Keyframes**: Bring your video to life with animations and dynamic effects to keep your audience engaged.

6. Review and Refine

- **Preview Your Work**: Play your video to ensure it flows seamlessly. Look for pacing or visual inconsistencies and make adjustments as needed.

- **Seek Feedback**: Share a draft with friends or colleagues for constructive input before finalizing.

7. Export and Share

- **Choose Export Settings**: Select the right resolution and format based on where you'll share your video—whether it's TikTok, YouTube, or another platform.

- **Save and Share**: Export your video and either save it locally or upload it directly from CapCut to your chosen platform.

8. Save for the Future

- **Backup Your Work**: Save a copy of your project files and the final exported video. You never know when you might want to revisit or repurpose it.

By planning, organizing, and making full use of CapCut's creative tools, you'll create videos that captivate and inspire your audience. Happy editing!

CHAPTER 2

EXPLORING THE CAPCUT USER INTERFACE

Welcome to Chapter Two! Here, we'll explore the foundation of your CapCut experience: its interface. Whether you're a first-time user or someone switching from another editing tool, mastering CapCut's layout is the first step toward creating amazing videos.

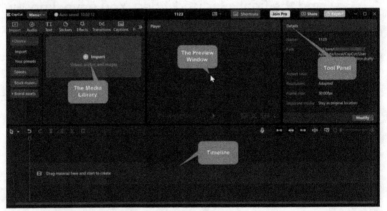

CapCut is celebrated for its clean, user-friendly design that caters to both beginners and pros. It's intuitive enough to help new users feel at ease but packed with features to satisfy advanced creators. This chapter will guide you through the essential parts of the interface, breaking down how each section works and how they all come together to make video editing a breeze.

We'll start with the basics—like importing your media and organizing your workspace—and then dive into the timeline, where the real magic happens. Along the way, you'll learn about the tools, panels, and settings that help you edit efficiently and creatively.

By the time you finish this chapter, you'll feel right at home in CapCut's interface, ready to take on any project with confidence and ease. Let's dive in and make editing simple, fun, and seamless!

What you will learn:

- A careful look at the interface segments
- Interface of CapCut mobile

A CAREFUL LOOK AT THE INTERFACE SEGMENTS

Let us look at various segments of the Window presented above. We will however talk about the physical segments and the other that can only be displayed via an event or action on them.

1. The Media Library:

All imported assets, such as audio files, photographs, and video clips, are saved in the media library.

The Media Library Features:

- **Drag & Drop**: Simply drag files into the library or timeline to move them there with ease.
- **Import Button**: Add media files directly from your device with a single click.
- **Organization Tools**: Keep your materials well-structured and accessible by utilizing tags and folders.

31

2. Timeline

The timeline is the most important part of your editing project. There, you assemble and manipulate your music files, video clips, and other media.

Key Features to Keep in Mind:

- **Playhead**: Move the playhead to different points in the timeline to review specific frames.
- **Tracks**: Arrange your video, audio, and overlay content across multiple levels for better organization.
- **Zoom In/Out**: Adjust the timeline's zoom to either make fine-tuned edits or see the full project at a glance.
- **Trim Handles**: Quickly adjust the start and end of a clip by dragging the trim handles.
- **Split Tool**: Split your video into two parts right at the playhead position with ease.

3. The Preview Window

The Preview Window enables you to view your work on the go, allowing you to see real-time changes as you edit.

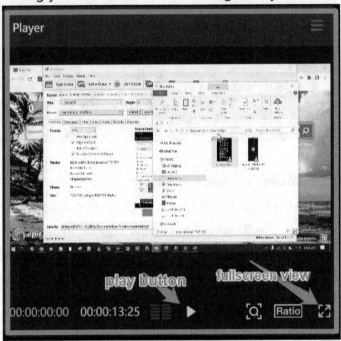

This feature is essential for ensuring accuracy and maintaining a smooth workflow. With the Preview Window, you can playback your edits, check transitions, effects, and audio synchronization, and ensure that your final product meets your vision. It provides a clear and dynamic view of your project, making it easier to spot and correct any mistakes instantly.

33

Key Features of the Preview Window

- **Full-Screen View**: Expand your view to full screen for a clearer and more detailed look at your edits.
- **Playback Controls**: Easily navigate through your video with options to play, pause, and fast-forward.

4. Exporting Media

The final step in your video editing journey with CapCut is exporting your project. This crucial step ensures your work is saved in a shareable format, making it ready for uploading to various platforms or sharing with your audience.

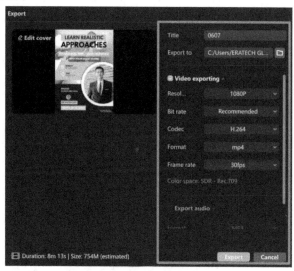

CapCut's Export Pane provides several options to optimize your video for the best viewing experience across different devices and platforms.

Key Features of the Export Pane

- **Resolution Settings**: Choose from multiple resolutions (e.g., 720p, 1080p, 4K) to match the quality requirements of your platform or audience. Adjusting resolution impacts file size and playback quality.

- **Frame Rate Selection**: Select frame rates (e.g., 24 fps, 30 fps, 60 fps) to control the smoothness of your video. Higher frame rates provide smoother motion, ideal for fast-paced or action content.

- **Format Options**: Export in standard formats like MP4, ensuring compatibility with most platforms and devices. Some versions of CapCut may offer additional formats for specific use cases.

- **Compression Settings**: Enable compression to reduce file size for easier uploading and sharing. Choose between high-quality and standard-quality compression options.

- **Custom Output Name and Location**: Rename your project and select the desired storage location for easy access post-export.
- **Platform-Specific Settings**: Optimize your video for specific platforms like YouTube, TikTok, or Instagram. Pre-adjusted settings ensure compliance with platform standards (e.g., aspect ratios, length).
- **Audio Settings**: Customize audio quality settings, including bitrate adjustments, to ensure sound clarity.

5. The Tool Panel

The Tool Panel is your comprehensive command center for video editing, offering an array of tools to fine-tune and elevate your content. Each feature is designed to enhance creativity and precision, ensuring a polished final product. Key tools include:

The Tool Panel

- **Cutout**: Trim and split clips with precision to refine the flow of your video and remove unnecessary portions.
- **Filters and Effects**: Apply artistic filters and eye-catching effects to give your video a unique aesthetic and enhance its visual appeal.
- **Adjustments**: Fine-tune brightness, contrast, saturation, and other visual properties to perfect your video's look and feel. These controls allow for subtle corrections or bold transformations.
- **Text and Titles**: Add captions, subtitles, or stylish text overlays to provide context, engage viewers, or emphasize key points. Choose from a variety of fonts, colors, and animations to match your style.

- **Animation**: Bring your video elements to life by adding motion to text, stickers, and graphics, making your content more engaging and dynamic.
- **Speed Adjustment**: Control playback speed to create dramatic slow-motion effects or accelerate for time-lapse sequences. This feature helps set the tone and pace of your narrative.
- **Audio Tools**: Seamlessly integrate music, sound effects, or voiceovers. Adjust volume levels, apply fade-in/out effects, and synchronize audio with visuals for a cohesive experience.
- **Chroma Key**: Unlock professional-grade green screen capabilities to replace backgrounds and transport your subjects to virtually any setting.

This versatile set of tools empowers you to craft videos that are not only visually stunning but also immersive and impactful.

INTERFACE OF CAPCUT MOBILE

The iOS and Android users can utilize CapCut's mobile interface, which is optimized for fluid video editing on smaller displays. Compared to the PC version, the layout is more straightforward, with a lower toolbar that makes it simple to access important functions like text, effects, audio, trimming, and transitions. While the video preview is shown above for in-the-moment modifications, users can organize and edit clips on the center timeline. The user experience is improved by touch motions for zooming and precision editing, which makes CapCut a simple and affordable option for video producers on both platforms.

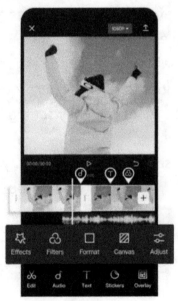

CHAPTER 3

STARTING YOUR EDITING JOURNEY IN CAPCUT

We are ready to move on to the most crucial stages of video production now that we have downloaded and installed CapCut and extensively examined its capabilities and interface. Planning and organizing the project, employing effective editing techniques, and adding the finishing touches to your film before exporting it will all be covered in this section. This chapter lays the foundation for transforming your ideas into polished, shareable creations using CapCut.

Whether your goal is to produce short films for social media, make cinematic classics, or experiment with imaginative storytelling, following these procedures will guarantee a polished, professional final result that is ready to be shared with your audience.

What you will learn:

- General procedure for video editing in CapCut
- How to access the CapCut app
- How to import media files into CapCut

- Organize or arrange your media files in CapCut
- Send media files to the timeline
- Arrange your clips on the timeline
- Editing your project
- Exporting and sharing your final product
- Guide on CapCut mobile

GENERAL PROCEDURE FOR VIDEO EDITING IN CAPCUT

To start editing in CapCut, the first step is to **import your media** files. This includes video clips, images, and audio, which can be uploaded to the Media Library. Once your files are imported, it's helpful to **organize them** by using folders and tags, making it easier to locate and manage your assets.

After organizing, **add your media to the timeline** by dragging and dropping files in the sequence you want. Use the trimming tools to **cut out unnecessary parts** of your clips and rearrange them to create a cohesive story. To make the transitions between scenes smoother, apply the built-in **transition effects** available in CapCut.

Next, enhance your video with creative elements. You can **apply filters and effects** to adjust the video's color tone or add overlays for a unique look. To add context or flair, use CapCut's tools to **insert text, subtitles, or stickers.**

Audio is another key element of video editing. Make sure to **sync your audio with the video**, adjust the volume levels, and add background music or sound effects to enrich the experience. Once your editing is complete, take the time to **preview your project** to ensure everything looks and sounds the way you want.

Finally, when you're satisfied with your work, **export the video** in the desired resolution and format. Your edited video is now ready to be shared or published on your chosen platform!

HOW TO ACCESS THE CAPCUT APP

Exciting times ahead! You're about to dive into the world of video editing with CapCut. This is the moment you've been waiting for – learning how to cut, trim, export, and share your creative work with the world. But before you begin, let's ensure you have everything you need for a smooth editing experience.

Things to Have Ready Before Starting Your Project in CapCut

1. Download and install the CapCut app on your mobile or desktop. Ensure it is updated to the latest version for the best features and performance.
2. Compile any video clip you intend to use. Prepare additional media like photos, background music, sound effects, and voiceovers.
3. Have a clear idea or storyboard of what you want to create. List any key transitions, effects, or edits you want to include.
4. Ensure there is enough free space on your device for editing and exporting.
5. If you plan to use CapCut's cloud-based features or download additional resources, a reliable internet connection is essential.
6. Spend a few minutes exploring the tools, timeline, and preview window. This will help you feel more confident as you begin editing.

7. Sit in a comfortable, distraction-free area. Use headphones for precise audio editing.

Once you've checked off everything from this list, you're ready to dive in and let your creativity shine! Happy editing!

To open CapCut Application follow these steps:
1. Open the Start Button and search for CapCut
2. Click to open it. You can decide to pin the icon to the taskbar if you so desire, for easy accessibility.

3. Once the App is opened to the initial window, Click Start to begin your project.

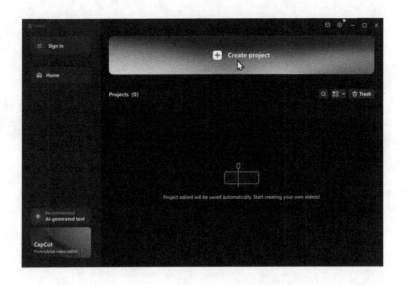

HOW TO IMPORT MEDIA FILES INTO CAPCUT

Importing your media assets is the initial step in any productive video editing procedure. Videos, pictures, audio files, and any other components you intend to employ in your project are examples of these assets. A more efficient workflow is ensured by properly importing and organizing your material, which makes it easier to find and use your files when editing. To help you build a solid foundation for your creative project, we'll walk you through the process of importing media files into CapCut in this part. Whether you're using the desktop or mobile version of CapCut, this tutorial will make sure your assets are prepared for use whenever inspiration strikes.

After completing this tutorial, your media files will be effectively imported and arranged, preparing you for a smooth editing process.

Importing Your Files:

CapCut has two primary ways to import media files. We will be looking at each of the methods. It will be left for you to decide which is easiest and you are comfortable with.

> ➢ Launch the CapCut application on your PC or mobile device.
> ➢ A new project can be started by clicking the "New Project" button on the main screen.
> ➢ The Media Library panel will show up on the left when the project workspace starts, organizing all of your imported media assets.

1: The button for importation:

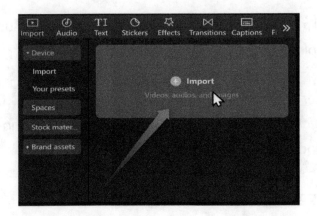

1. In the Media Library window, click the "Import" button to open a file browser.
2. Navigate to the location where your media files are stored on your device.
3. Select the files you want to import and click "Open." The chosen files will now appear in the Media Library.

2: The Click and Drag Method:

Find and open the folder on your computer that contains your media files. From the folder, drag and drop the chosen files directly into CapCut's Media Library panel.

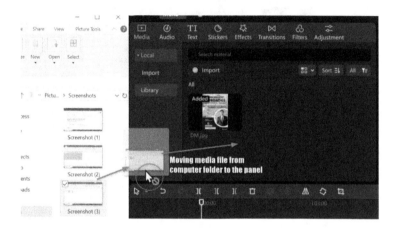

You can also use the menu option just above the Media Pane. To do that simply click the menu to access the File options, and from the list select between the New Project, or Import to locate your media file.

ORGANIZE OR ARRANGE YOUR MEDIA FILES IN CAPCUT

Efficiently organizing your media in CapCut helps streamline your workflow and keeps your project tidy. Follow these steps to manage your files effectively:

1. Import your files into CapCut's Media Library – videos, images, and audio files.

2. Right-click on the Media Library panel and select **"New Folder"** from the dropdown menu.

3. Name the folder descriptively for easy identification.

- Use specific names, such as *"Audio Files," "Video Clips,"* or *"Background Images,"* to make locating files easier.

- Avoid generic names like *"Folder 1"* to prevent confusion, especially in larger projects.

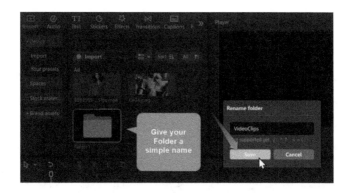

4. Drag and drop your media files into the relevant folders.

5. Apply tags to your media files for additional categorization and searchability, if needed.

Another exciting thing about media organization in CapCut is that you can Sort or Filter your Media Items Imported to the Media Window for easy accessibility. Do it by right-clicking the Media Window, and you will see the options available for you.

Tips for Managing Your Media Effectively

1. **Use Clear Names:** Rename your files and folders with descriptive names, like "Vacation Photos" or "Project Audio," so they are easy to find.
2. **Add Tags:** Organize your media by category using tags like "Video Clips," "Images," or "Audio." This makes it simple to sort and locate files.

3. **Keep Backups:** Always save backup copies of your files in a separate location to protect your work from accidental loss.

SEND MEDIA FILES TO THE TIMELINE

You've succeeded in organizing your media files and folders. Now is the time to move to the drawing board – the Timeline. The Timeline collects all the media files that you've chosen to work with per time.

We have again two ways to fly your files into the Timeline – by dragging and dropping, or using the plus ✛ sign attached to individual media files. To move any file, see the illustration below:

1. **Drag and Drop File:** You can drag and drop your media files to the Timeline one after the other or in bulk by selecting the required files before moving them to the Timeline.
2. **Using the plus ✛ sign**, you can quickly add your files to the Timeline.

ARRANGE YOUR CLIPS ON THE TIMELINE

One of the most important steps in creating the flow of your video is organizing the clips on the timeline. Start by placing the clips in the order you want them to appear in your final project. If you need to adjust the sequence, simply drag and drop the clips to reposition them.

You can also split or trim clips to remove unnecessary parts and align them with your story or message. Pay attention to the transitions between clips to ensure the flow feels natural. Consider adding overlapping clips, such as B-roll footage, for dynamic visuals.

Organizing your timeline effectively helps create a clear structure, making it easier to focus on other aspects like effects, audio, and text additions. A well-arranged timeline sets the foundation for a professional and engaging video.

EDITING YOUR PROJECT

To assist you in creating an engaging and distinctive video, CapCut offers a wide range of editing options, such as text, effects, transitions, and clip-splitting. This step is essential, as it highlights your creative and technical skills in media editing, ultimately influencing the quality and impact of your final work.

Spend some time exploring and making good use of the options that are accessible. Use effects to improve your video's aesthetic appeal and style, transitions to guarantee smooth scene changes, and text to convey important information.

Regularly use the **preview or play function** to review your edits and ensure all elements work harmoniously. Attention to detail during this process is essential for producing a polished, professional result that leaves a lasting impression.

EXPORTING AND SHARING YOUR FINAL PRODUCT

When your video is complete and ready to share, click on the **Export** button. Choose your desired resolution and other export settings to ensure the best quality for your project. Once the export process is complete, you can save the video to your device or upload it directly to your preferred social media platform.

By carefully selecting the right settings, you ensure that your video looks its best, whether it's shared online or saved for personal use.

Tips for Exporting and Sharing Your Final Product

1. Choose a compatible file format like MP4 for smooth playback.
2. Adjust resolution, frame rate, and bitrate to balance quality and file size.
3. Use the correct video dimensions for different platforms (e.g., 9:16 for TikTok, and 16:9 for YouTube).
4. Create an attractive thumbnail if the platform allows it.
5. Watch the exported video to check for any errors or glitches.
6. Keep copies of your video in multiple locations for backup.

58

GUIDE ON CAPCUT MOBILE

CapCut Mobile offers a powerful yet user-friendly video editing experience right from your smartphone. This guide will walk you through essential steps to help you create professional-quality videos on the go. From importing your media to exporting your final product, you'll learn how to effectively use CapCut's features to bring your creative ideas to life Using Mobile Devices. Let's dive in!

Launch the CapCut app on your smartphone to get started:

When you activate the app, the home screen will appear with several options. Then, to begin a new project, tap the "Create Project" button.

Importing your media comes next after you've started your project. By choosing the appropriate files from your device, you can import your audio, video, or picture files. After being uploaded to your project, these resources will be prepared for modification.

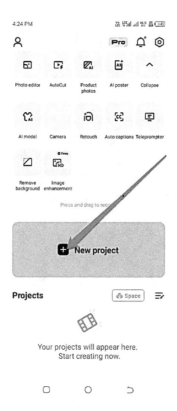

Organize Media Clips:

On your video timeline, choose the sequence in which you want the imported media files to appear. Pressing down on a clip will move them across the timeline and modify their order.

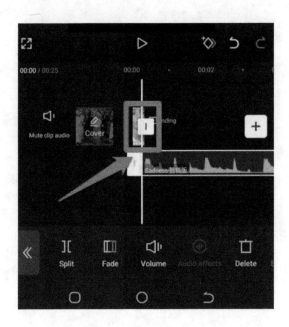

Start Editing Your Work:

CapCut provides a wide range of editing tools, including text, effects, transitions, and clip splitting, which you can use to enhance your video and make it truly unique. This stage is particularly important because it is where you'll demonstrate your ability to manipulate and refine your media. The decisions you make here will directly influence the quality and impact of your final video.

To achieve the best result, take the time to explore each tool and understand how it can improve your project. For example, use text to convey key information, apply transitions to ensure smooth scene changes, and experiment with effects to add visual appeal. Splitting clips allows you to refine your footage by cutting out unnecessary parts, so your video flows naturally.

By carefully utilizing the available tools and features, you can create a well-edited video that stands out and effectively communicates your message.

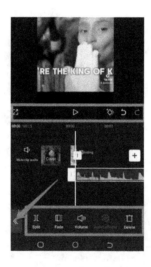

Preview, Export, and Share Your Video:

Make the most of the preview or play button to review your edits. Once your clips are arranged and refined, finalize your project by ensuring everything looks and sounds as intended with a thorough preview.

When ready, click the export button and use the top-right arrow to save and share your final project effortlessly.

CHAPTER 4:

CUSTOMIZING YOUR WORKSPACE

We will delve into the art of making CapCut truly your own. A well-organized and personalized workspace can significantly boost your efficiency and creativity. In this chapter, you'll briefly learn how to customize the interface, adjust settings to fit your workflow and unlock tools that align with your editing style. Gaining proficiency with these tweaks will increase your output and make the process of editing videos easier and more pleasurable.

What you will learn:

- Layout customization
- Using a computer to set up the video aspect ratio (the video screen size)
- Customizing CapCut mobile

LAYOUT CUSTOMIZATION

CapCut is a full-featured video editing program that offers several cutting-edge tools to improve the editing experience. By making these tools easily accessible through the user-friendly interface, creators may increase editing speed and produce videos of professional quality. The following outlines some key features and how to configure them:

Multiple Languages Customization

CapCut offers a multilingual interface, making it easier for users worldwide to edit in their native language. You can change language by following these steps:

1. Locate the Menu tab at the top left and select the "Settings" option.
2. Tap "Language."
3. Select your preferred language from the options.
4. Confirm to switch the interface language.

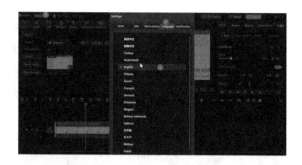

Deciding Output Resolution, Frame Rate, Or Bitrate for Video:

Choosing the right output resolution in CapCut is crucial for ensuring your video looks its best on the intended platform. Higher resolutions like 1080p or 4K offer superior clarity but may require more storage space and processing power. Lower resolutions, such as 720p, are ideal for faster uploads or when targeting devices with smaller screens. To set the output resolution in CapCut:

1. Tap the **Export** button after finishing your edit.
2. Select your preferred resolution from the options (e.g., 720p, 1080p, or 4K).
3. Adjust additional settings, like frame rate or bitrate, if needed.

Matching the resolution to your platform and audience's needs ensures optimal viewing quality.

Accessing The Shortcut Menu:

CapCut's shortcut menu is intended to help users expedite their workflow by giving them instant access to often-used editing features. With only a few taps, editors can divide, duplicate, delete, or modify clips thanks to this function, which cuts down on the amount of time they spend traversing the program. It is a necessary tool for accurate and effective video editing.

To access the menu simply hover top-right and the menu will appear with options to select from different tabs. See the screenshot below:

Setting Up the CapCut Layout:

For a smooth and effective editing experience, you must set up the CapCut layout. In this tutorial, we'll go over the fundamentals of workspace organization to help you get the most out of your work.

Why Setting Up Your Layout Matters

A well-organized layout ensures:

- Easy access to features and tools.

- Smooth workflow for editing videos.
- Better focus and creativity.

To change or switch between layout styles, hover to the top-right, where you'll see the layout button, as shown here. Select the best option that you like. Observe the display while you navigate through the options.

Making sure your setup is successful is essential before you start using CapCut on your device to edit videos creatively. This section will walk you through the basic procedures to get the most out of CapCut, such as customizing necessary settings and setting up your media.

USING A COMPUTER TO SET UP THE VIDEO ASPECT RATIO (THE VIDEO SCREEN SIZE)

What is the Aspect Ratio of a Video?

The aspect ratio of a video is the proportional relationship between its width and height, expressed as two numbers separated by a colon (e.g., 16:9, 4:3). For instance, a 16:9 aspect ratio is commonly used for widescreen content like YouTube videos or modern TV displays, while a 4:3 ratio is typical for older television screens. This ratio affects the composition, visual appeal, and how the video appears on different screens.

What is the Aspect Ratio of a Video?

The aspect ratio of a video is the proportional relationship between its width and height, expressed as two numbers separated by a colon (e.g., 16:9, 4:3). For instance, a 16:9 aspect ratio is commonly used for widescreen content like YouTube videos or modern TV displays, while a 4:3 ratio is typical for older television screens. This ratio affects the composition, visual appeal, and how the video appears on different screens.

Types of Video Screen and Application:

- **Widescreen (16:9):** Widely used for HDTVs, YouTube videos, modern TV shows, and most computer monitors.
- **Standard (4:3):** Traditional ratio for older TVs, classic shows, and vintage media.
- **Square (1:1):** Ideal for social media platforms like Instagram.
- **Vertical (9:16):** Popular for mobile content on Snapchat, TikTok, and Instagram Stories.
- **Cinematic (21:9):** Extra-wide ratio used in films and high-end monitors for an immersive experience.

Selecting the Best Aspect Ratio:

- **Content-Type:** Define the objective of your video, whether it's for a tutorial, social media, or a film.
- **Platform Guidelines:** Check the platform or device's recommended aspect ratio for proper display.
- **Visual Design and Composition:** Plan the layout and framing of your subjects to achieve the best visual effect

How to Adjust Video Screen Size or Aspect Ratio in CapCut PC

- **Start a New Project:** For editing, click "New Project" or "Create New Project" after opening CapCut.

- **Import Your Videos:** The video file you wish to edit can be uploaded by clicking the "Import" button. The aspect ratio for this example will be set to 9:16, which is perfect for mobile platforms like YouTube Shorts and TikTok.

- **Set the Aspect Ratio:** Find the "Aspect Ratio" option, usually in the settings or project options, once your video has appeared in the timeline or preview window. Decide on the ratio you want.

- **Adjust and Confirm:** To fit the selected aspect ratio, the canvas will resize. Use the preview pane to scale or move your video if needed. To get the ideal fit, drag the clip's edges to change its alignment.

EXPORTING YOUR PROJECT IN CAPCUT

Once you've completed editing, the last action is to export your video. Exporting allows you to save your project in a format suitable for sharing across various platforms. Follow these steps to seamlessly export your video:

1. In the top right corner of the CapCut screen, click the "**Export**" button. This will open the window with the export settings.

74

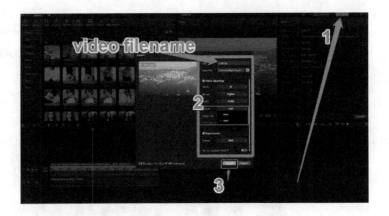

Configure Export Settings:

- **Resolution:** Depending on the quality you require and the capabilities of your source footage, select the resolution. For instance, 4K is perfect for ultra-high-resolution information, which offers remarkable clarity but requires more storage space, whereas 1080p is frequently used for high-quality videos.

- **Frame Rate:** The smoothness of your movie depends on the frame rate. Standard frame rates are 30 frames per second (fps) for everyday videos, 60 fps for high-motion content like fast action or sports, and 24 fps for a cinematic effect. Select the option that best suits your video's style and desired level of quality.

- **Format:** Choose the file format that best suits your requirements. MP4 is the most popular format because it effectively balances file size and video quality, making it perfect for cross-platform sharing.
- **Quality:** According to your demands, change the quality parameters. Because higher quality settings led to bigger file sizes, before choosing a better-quality choice, take platform compatibility and storage into account.
- **Export Path:** To save the exported video, select a destination folder on your device. Based on your resolution and quality options, make sure you have adequate storage space to hold the final file size.

Exporting Your Video

- **Start Exporting:** After configuring your settings, click the "Export" button to begin the process.
- **Monitor Progress:** The export progress will be shown through a progress bar. The time it takes will depend on factors like the video length and chosen export options.
- **Completion:** Once the export is finished, you'll receive a notification, and your video will be saved in the specified folder for you to access.

Additional Export Features:

CapCut offers the option to directly publish your video to platforms such as YouTube, Instagram, and TikTok. Just choose your desired platform and follow the prompts to upload. Familiarizing yourself with the export settings ensures that your video retains its high definition and is optimized for the platform's requirements. Once exported, you're all set to showcase your creation to the world!

CUSTOMIZING CAPCUT MOBILE

Video Resolutions, Frame Rate, And Code Rate

CapCut offers customizable video settings, allowing you to achieve the best performance and quality tailored to your needs. You can adjust your mobile device's resolution, frame rate, and bitrate (Mbps) with ease:

To optimize your video, choose a resolution (480p, 720p, or 1080p) based on project or platform needs, and select a frame rate (24 fps for cinematic effects, 60 fps for smoother motion). Adjust the "Code Rate" or "Bit Rate" to balance video quality and file size, prioritizing the recommended settings for optimal results.

Getting Rid of The Video Watermark or The Project's Default Ending

Watermarks and default endings, frequently embedded by free video editing platforms like CapCut, can significantly impact the professional appearance and overall quality of a finely edited video.

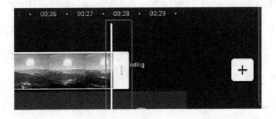

This section will show you how to remove watermarks and default endings from your films so that the finished product is clean and professional. Steps to remove the default ending:

1. Click settings from the start-up window.

2. To delete it, toggle the Add default ending option from the options menu, then confirm your selection and exit the window.

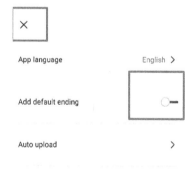

The default closing clip with the CapCut icon will never appear on your project once you unhook the button.

Now that you have gotten the know-how of the nitty-gritty of CapCut, is time to explore the Ticks & Tips in CapCut Video Production, and then begin exploring advanced Video Editing Techniques as used by Movie Production Companies.

CHAPTER 5

FUNDAMENTAL CAPCUT EDITING TECHNIQUES

This chapter serves as your essential guide to mastering CapCut's tools and features, empowering you to unlock your full creative potential. Learn how to craft compelling stories with ease, leveraging CapCut's versatile effects, seamless transitions, and precision clip-cutting tools. You'll also explore advanced techniques for organizing your footage, refining visual elements, and enhancing audio to create videos that truly stand out. Whether you're a beginner or refining your skills, these techniques will equip you to produce professional-quality content with confidence.

What You'll Learn:

- Video and audio clips trimming and splitting
- Knowing how to use transitions and visual effects
- How to include video and body effects in your projects
- Using CapCut Desktop to apply trending video effects

- Applying light dissolves body effects on CapCut mobile
- Amazing video filters to create stunning videos
- Applications for amusing stickers in videos

VIDEO AND AUDIO CLIPS TRIMMING AND SPLITTING

A video can be split into smaller portions for more precise editing while trimming removes extraneous footage from the beginning or finish of the film. Throughout your editing process, you'll make use of these features.

How to Time or Split Video Clip:

Select the Video Clip: Begin by selecting the video clip from the timeline that you wish to edit. This step allows you to focus on the specific segment you want to modify.

Use the "Split" Tool: To divide the clip into smaller sections, use the "Split" tool. Alternatively, you can adjust the length of the clip by dragging the handles on either side, enabling precise edits to fit your desired outcome.

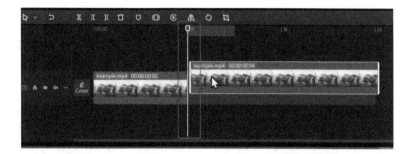

Trim or Delete Unwanted Sections: Remove unnecessary parts of the clip by dragging its edges to shrink unwanted portions. For quicker edits, utilize the "Delete Left" or "Delete Right" features to efficiently eliminate specific sections.

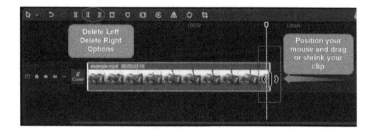

Directive: Follow these steps to refine your video clips and achieve seamless edits. Refer to the accompanying screenshot for additional clarity.

How to Time or Split Audio Clips:

1. From your device, import your audio clip.

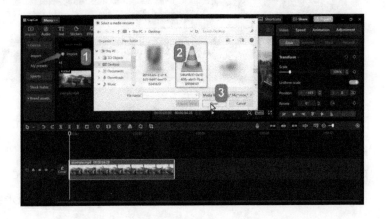

2. From the timeline, pick the audio clip.

3. To change the clip's length, use the handles on either side or use the "Split" tool to split it into smaller parts.

Insights: You may occasionally get more accuracy by using the trim handles at the edge of the clips because the preview pane will move with your actions on the clip. You can use this to easily determine where to stop or continue. You simply need to pay closer attention when cutting the clips. You need to make sure that the timing of your audio and video is correct.

KNOWING HOW TO USE TRANSITIONS AND VISUAL EFFECTS

1. Understanding and Using Transitions

Transitions are essential for smoothly connecting different clips or scenes, ensuring a cohesive flow in your video narrative. They help maintain the viewer's attention by creating seamless progressions between segments, enhancing the overall storytelling experience. Mastering the use of transitions in CapCut allows you to blend diverse material effortlessly, enabling a polished and professional feel. Properly applied transitions ensure that each scene complements the next, keeping the narrative engaging and visually coherent.

Transition types in CapCut:

CapCut offers a variety of transition types to enhance the flow and style of your videos. These transitions help create seamless connections between clips, ensuring a professional and visually appealing result. Here's an overview of the main transition types available in CapCut:

- **Basic Transitions:** These include simple fades, dissolves, and cuts that provide clean and smooth transitions. They are ideal for maintaining a subtle and polished look in professional projects.
- **Dynamic Transitions:** Dynamic transitions like zooms, spins, and wipes add energy and motion to your video. They are great for action-packed scenes or to emphasize dramatic shifts between clips.
- **3D Transitions:** These transitions utilize three-dimensional effects such as flips, rotations, and cube transitions to add depth and a modern aesthetic to your videos.
- **Overlay Transitions:** Overlay transitions use visual elements like light leaks, flares, or color overlays to enhance the visual appeal of the clip changes. They're perfect for adding a creative or cinematic touch.
- **Thematic Transitions:** CapCut also includes thematic transitions tailored for specific moods or

genres, such as glitch effects for futuristic content or vintage-inspired transitions for a retro look.

- **Custom Transitions:** With CapCut's advanced tools, you can create custom transitions by combining effects, motion, and animation for a unique, personalized touch that aligns with your creative vision.

CapCut Transition Effects:

1. **Blur:** The current clip gradually loses focus and becomes blurry before the next clip appears in sharp

clarity. This transition is great for adding a dreamy or subtle effect to your video, making it feel smoother and less abrupt.

2. **Bounce:** Clips switch with a bouncy motion, mimicking the springy movement of an object. This effect works particularly well for playful, lighthearted, or animated content, adding a fun and energetic vibe.

3. **Clock Wipe:** The next clip enters the frame in a circular motion, similar to how the hands of a clock move. This effect adds a sense of continuity and works well in thematic storytelling or when emphasizing the passage of time.

4. **Cube:** The current clip rotates off-screen as though it's on one face of a cube, revealing the next clip on an adjacent face. This dynamic 3D effect adds depth and modernity to your transitions, making them visually engaging.

5. **Dissolve:** The first clip fades into the next, blending the two seamlessly. Often used in emotional or cinematic

scenes, this transition enhances the storytelling flow and creates a soft, polished look.

6. **Fade In/Out:** The screen gradually darkens to black (fade out) or lightens from black (fade in). It's a classic and versatile transition, ideal for starting or ending your video or marking a significant pause or scene change.

7. **Fade to Color:** This transition allows your clip to fade into a solid color, such as white or any customizable hue, before transitioning to the next. It's useful for creating chapter breaks, emphasizing mood changes, or adding a professional touch.

8. **Flip:** One clip flip over like a turning page, revealing the next clip on the reverse side. This transition works well for slideshow presentations, travel videos, or storytelling with a nostalgic or scrapbook-like feel.

9. **Glitch:** This edgy transition mimics the effect of digital interference or static. It's perfect for tech-inspired, futuristic, or music videos, giving them a bold and modern aesthetic.

10. **Light Flash:** A sudden flash of bright light obscures the screen momentarily before revealing the next clip. This dramatic effect is ideal for action-packed sequences, transitions in trailers, or highlighting a climactic moment.

11. **Ripple:** As one clip transitions to the next, a wave-like ripple effect appears on the screen, as though a stone has been dropped into water. This effect adds a calming, fluid motion and is excellent for nature or relaxation-themed content.

12. **Shape Transitions:** Geometric shapes (such as circles, stars, or rectangles) expand, contract, or shift to reveal the next clip. These transitions bring a playful and creative element, making them ideal for kids' videos, artistic projects, or branding content.

13. **Slice:** The screen appears to be sliced into sections, with one clip transitioning to another through diagonal, vertical, or horizontal cuts. This sharp and dynamic transition suits edgy or high-energy videos, like sports or action edits.

14. **Slide:** The current clip moves out of the frame while the next clip slides in from a specified direction (e.g., left, right, up, or down). This classic transition style is versatile and works well for professional, casual, or themed videos.

15. **Spin:** One clip spins out of view while the next spins in, creating a rotational motion that feels dynamic and engaging. Ideal for travel, dance, or energetic videos, this transition can add excitement to your edits.

16. **Wipe:** The next clip seems to wipe away the current one, often in a specific direction or pattern (e.g., left to right or top to bottom). This transition is simple yet effective for keeping the narrative flow smooth and visually appealing.

17. **Zoom:** The transition mimics a zoom-in or zoom-out effect, moving between clips as if focusing in or out of a picture. This cinematic effect adds a polished touch, perfect for professional projects or videos with storytelling elements.

Tips for Using Transitions Effectively

- Match the transition type with the theme and tone of your video. For instance, "Glitch" works well for tech or sci-fi projects, while "Fade In/Out" suits emotional or cinematic moments.
- Experiment with transition speeds to find the right pacing. A faster transition adds energy, while a slower one feels more dramatic or relaxed.
- Use transitions sparingly; overusing them can make your video appear cluttered or overly complex.

How to Include Transition Effects:

Adding transition effects is an essential step in creating seamless and visually engaging videos. To start, select your video clips, and tap on the **"Transitions"** tab in the CapCut interface. This opens a variety of transition options to choose from, including fades, slides, and dynamic effects like spins and ripples. Once you've selected your desired effect, you can apply it by dragging it into the timeline between two clips or by tapping the **"+"** sign on the transition effect for automatic placement.

If your video consists of one continuous clip and you wish to add transitions within it, use the **"Split"** tool to divide the video into sections. Splitting your clips allows you to insert transitions between specific scenes or moments, giving your project a more professional and polished look.

After adding the transition, fine-tune its duration by dragging its edges in the timeline. Adjusting the timing ensures the transition feels natural and aligns with the rhythm of your video. By following these steps, you can effectively incorporate transitions to enhance the flow and storytelling in your content.

Using and Modifying Multiple Transitions in CapCut:

With CapCut, applying and modifying many transitions is a simple procedure that enables you to produce a polished and well-organized video. Here's the method:

1. Choose Clips for Transitions

- Start by selecting the clip where you want to add a transition.
- If you're working with multiple clips, you can select the spaces between the clips on the timeline where transitions will be applied.

2. Apply Transitions

- Tap on the **"Transitions"** tab and browse the available effects.
- Hover over the desired transition and apply it by either dragging it to the transition point between two clips or tapping the **"+"** button to add it.
- Repeat this process for additional clips where transitions are needed.

3. Modify Transitions

- Once added, you can adjust the duration or speed of each transition by selecting it in the timeline and dragging its edges.
- Experiment with different styles and timings to ensure the transitions match your video's tone and flow.

Making changes to a transition will change how long it lasts and how long it takes in your video.

By selecting and customizing transitions across multiple clips, you can enhance the visual storytelling of your video while maintaining consistency and professionalism.

2. Mastering Visual Effects

Visual effects are powerful tools for adding creativity, flair, and impact to your videos. These effects can highlight key moments, evoke emotions, or simply make your content more visually appealing. In CapCut, proficiency with video effects allow you to enhance the brightness, tone, and mood of your footage, making it more engaging and memorable. Whether you're aiming for a dramatic highlight or a subtle aesthetic enhancement, visual effects offer endless possibilities to elevate the quality of your work.

CapCut Video and Body Effects

CapCut offers a wide range of **video and body effects** that transform ordinary footage into visually captivating content, helping you enhance your storytelling and engage your audience. These effects give editors the creative tools they need to give their projects distinctive looks and moods.

Video Effects:
Video effects give your clips flair and energy, transforming ordinary footage into eye-catching entertainment. CapCut comprises several categories, including:

Video Effects Categories:

1. **Trending:** Effects that are popular and commonly used by creators for a contemporary or viral appeal.

2. **Opening & Closing:** Specific effects are designed to enhance the start or end of a video, giving a professional or dramatic touch.

3. **Nightclub:** Dynamic, vibrant effects are often associated with party or club scenes, such as strobes and neon lights.

4. **Lens:** Camera-inspired effects that simulate lens flares, focus changes, or zooms to mimic real-life photography and videography.
5. **Retro:** Nostalgic filters or overlays that give videos a vintage or old-school vibe, such as grainy film effects.
6. **Light Effects:** Effects that incorporate beams, glows, or sparkling lights to enhance the brightness and liveliness of a video.
7. **Glitch:** Digital distortion effects that simulate errors or futuristic aesthetics are often used in sci-fi or tech-themed videos.

There are other Video effects other than the ones mentioned here. Take your time and explore more from the menu.

Individual Effects Displayed Under Trending: The following Effects are sub-categories of the Trending Effects. Each of the listed categories has its sub-categories under it, to be applied to your videos.

- **Blur:** Smoothly blurs the video or parts of it, drawing focus to specific elements or creating a dreamy effect.

- **Explosion:** Adds an animated burst of energy or light, often used for dramatic impact.
- **Zoom Lens:** Mimics the effect of zooming in or out on the subject, creating a dynamic motion.
- **Mini Zoom:** A subtler zoom effect that focuses on a smaller area for emphasis.
- **Color Glow:** Adds vibrant, glowing color overlays that can evoke a psychedelic or energetic vibe.
- **Heart Kisses:** Creates an overlay of animated hearts, adding a playful or romantic touch to the scene.

How to Use These Effects in CapCut:

1. Navigate to the **Effects** tab in the CapCut editor, after selecting the clip to be applied.
2. Choose a category (e.g., Trending, Retro, etc.) that aligns with your video's theme.
3. Browse the effects, select one, and tap to apply it to your clip.
4. Adjust the effect's intensity, position, and duration for a seamless integration with your video.

Body Effects:

Body effects are intended to offer stylish additions to your film while focusing on specific individuals or subjects. Here are a few instances:

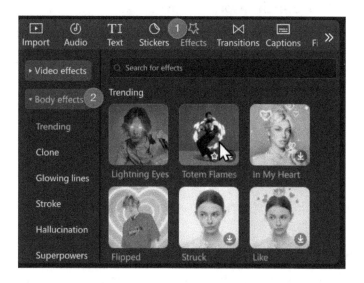

Body Effects Categories:

1. **Trending:** Popular body effects are frequently used by creators to enhance videos with attention-grabbing visuals.
2. **Clone:** Effects that replicate or duplicate a subject within the frame, adding a surreal or sci-fi element.

3. **Glowing Lines:** Stylish glowing outlines or patterns around the subject, often used to emphasize motion or a dynamic appearance.
4. **Stroke:** Adds bold outlines or accents around the subject, giving a cartoonish or graphic touch.
5. **Hallucination:** Surreal effects that distort or manipulate the subject, creating dreamlike or psychedelic visuals.
6. **Superpowers:** Fantasy effects that simulate supernatural abilities, such as fire, lightning, or energy waves.

There are other body effects other than the ones mentioned here. Take your time and explore more from the menu.

Individual Effects Displayed: Each of the listed categories has its sub-categories under it, to be applied to your videos.

- **Lightning Eyes:** Adds glowing, electrified effects around the subject's eyes, giving a powerful or intense appearance.
- **Totem Flames:** Surrounds the subject with swirling flames or fire-like visuals, creating a dramatic or energetic vibe.

- **In My Heart:** Overlay of soft, romantic elements like hearts, ideal for love-themed or emotional content.
- **Flipped:** A rotating or mirroring effect that distorts the subject in a playful or surreal way.
- **Struck:** Adds an animated element, such as lightning or other striking visuals, emphasizing intensity or drama.
- **Like Effect:** Enhances the picture with symbols like hearts or emojis, making it ideal for humorous or social media-friendly content.

How to Use Body Effects in CapCut:
1. Navigate to the **Effects** tab and select **Body Effects,** after selecting the clip to be applied.
2. Choose a category based on your video's theme or creative vision (e.g., Trending, Superpowers).
3. Select an effect and tap to apply it to the subject in your clip.
4. Customize the effect by adjusting its intensity, placement, and duration.

Tips for Effective Use of Body Effects:
- **Match Effects to the Video's Mood:** Use romantic effects like **In My Heart** for emotional content or intense effects like **Lightning Eyes** for dramatic scenes.

- **Avoid Overuse:** Focus on enhancing key moments to maintain a professional look.
- **Experiment with Combinations:** Combine body effects with video effects (e.g., light glows or transitions) for a layered and unique outcome.

With the help of CapCut's Body Effects, you can create videos that enthrall and amuse your viewers by incorporating unique possibilities for impact and personality.

How to Include Video and Body Effects in your Projects:

To include any of the mentioned effects follow the steps here:

1. **Select the Clip:** Tap on the video clip in your timeline.
2. **Open the Effects Tab:** Navigate to either **Video Effects** or **Body Effects** from the menu.
3. **Choose an Effect:** Browse through the categories and pick one that complements your project.
4. **Adjust Intensity and Duration:** Customize the effect to match the timing and tone of your video for a seamless result.

HOW TO INCLUDE VIDEO AND BODY EFFECTS IN YOUR PROJECTS

To include any of the mentioned effects follow the steps here. These steps are just a guide for you to prepare your mind ahead of the practical sessions to be discussed later.

1. Select the Clip

Begin by tapping on the video clip in your timeline to highlight it. Ensure the specific clip you want to enhance is selected since effects will only apply to the active clip. If your project includes multiple clips, you can apply effects individually to each section or layer them across clips for a more cohesive appearance.

2. Open the Effects Tab

Tap on the **"Effects"** icon in the menu bar at the bottom of the screen. From here, navigate to either **Video Effects** or **Body Effects** based on your creative goals. Video effects are ideal for modifying the entire frame, and setting the tone or mood of the video, while body effects are best for enhancing the subjects within the frame with dynamic or thematic elements.

3. Choose an Effect

Explore the categorized effects in the library, such as **Trending**, **Retro**, or **Superpowers**. Tap on an effect to preview how it looks on your clip and select the one that aligns with your creative vision. For example, use **Color Glow** for a romantic feel or **Lightning Eyes** to add a dramatic flair. Experiment with different options, but ensure the effects complement the overall theme of your project.

4. Adjust Intensity and Duration

After applying an effect, customize it by tapping on it in the timeline. Adjust the **intensity** to make the effect more subtle or pronounced, depending on the mood of your video. Modify the **duration** to synchronize the effect with key moments in your clip. Proper adjustments ensure the effects enhance your video without becoming distracting or overpowering.

5. Preview the Effects

Always preview the applied effects before finalizing your project. Play the video from the timeline to check how the effect integrates with the clip and ensure it flows naturally within the scene. Make additional adjustments if necessary to improve timing, intensity, or overall fit.

Additional Tips

- **Blend Effects Seamlessly:** Combine effects and transitions to produce edits that are fluid and appear professional.
- **Layer Effects for Creativity:** For depth, combine body effects and video, such as using vintage filters with glowing outlines.

By following these procedures, you can optimize CapCut's body effects and video effects and make sure your project is polished and captivating.

USING CAPCUT DESKTOP TO APPLY TRENDING VIDEO EFFECTS

CapCut's desktop version provides an impressive selection of trending video effects that elevate your footage and give it a modern, professional touch. This section will guide you through three popular and widely used effects: **Lens**, **Vlog Effects**, and **Glitch**. These effects are versatile and ideal for creating dynamic, eye-catching content. Let's explore how to apply them effectively!

1. Utilizing CapCut's Lens Effect

The Lens Effect in CapCut may add a distinctive and dramatic touch to your videos by simulating many camera lenses. The following is how to apply and modify this effect:

Steps to Apply the Lens Effect in CapCut Desktop

1. **Create a New Project**: Open CapCut and click on the "+" icon to start a new project. Import the video clip you want to edit by selecting your media file from your computer. (We have talked about these; you can reference them if you've forgotten)
2. **Add the Clip to the Timeline**: Drag and drop the imported video onto the timeline to begin editing.
3. **Select the Video Clip**: Click on the video in the timeline to activate it for editing.
4. **Access the Effects Panel**: Navigate to the top-left corner of the screen and click on the **"Effects"** button.
5. **Locate the Lens Effects**: In the Effects menu, find the **Lens** category and open it. Browse through the available options and select your desired lens effect.

6. **Apply the Fisheye-3 Effect**: For this example, choose the **Fisheye-3** effect to add a unique, curved distortion to your video for a bold and creative touch.

The numbering illustrates the process from the point of selecting the clip you wish to add the effect to the preview of the effect.

This is the effect's full-screen view. You can experiment with more lens effects at your own pace. Preview any changes you applied to your project on a large screen.

Modifying the Lens Effect Settings in CapCut

CapCut allows you to customize lens effects by adjusting settings like **Filters**, **Strength**, and **Twist** to fit your creative needs. Here's how to modify the lens effect:

1. **Select the Clip**: Choose the video clip in your timeline and position the playhead where you want to apply the effect.

2. **Apply the Effect**: In the **Effects** pane, find the **Lens Effects** category, select your preferred effect, and click the "**+**" sign to apply it.

3. **Adjust Settings**: With the clip selected, go to the top-right **Settings** or **Edit Window** to modify parameters

such as **Filters**, **Strength**, and **Twist** to achieve the desired effect.

Make sure the effects are exactly what you want before finishing your project. You may preview it to see it in real-time and change the clip length. By following these instructions, you can customize the lens effect and increase the visual impact of your film.

2. Utilizing CapCut's Vlog Effects:

Give your vlogs a unique flair by adding creative vlog effects. Here's how to apply and customize them in CapCut:

1. Import your video clips into the app.
2. Drag them onto the timeline.

3. Choose the specific clip where you'd like to add an effect.
4. Remember, you can apply multiple effects to one clip or use different effects on various clips.
5. Go to the effects menu and select the *Vlog* option.
6. Pick the *Car Window* effect (as shown below).
7. Fine-tune the effect settings and preview your changes.

You can follow the same procedures listed earlier to adjust and blend your effects.

Applying the Chromo-Zoom Glitch Effect:

The Chromo-Zoom effect in the Glitch category on CapCut adds a dynamic, glitchy aesthetic to your videos, perfect for creating dramatic transitions. How to master this effect is as follows:

1. Select the clip on the timeline where you want to apply the effect.
2. Tap the "Effects" button at the top of the screen.
3. In the left pane, browse or search through the available effect categories and choose *Glitch*.
4. Tap on *Glitch* to explore the various glitch effects, and select the *Chromo-Zoom* effect.
5. Press "+" to give your footage the Glitch effect. The application may take a while to download.

You may precisely customize the effect's duration and appearance by resizing or adjusting its length on the timeline to your preferences. This adaptability enables you to adjust the effect's timing to improve the impact and flow of your film.

This is a preview of the chromo-zoom effect in widescreen mode.

Body Effects in Video Applications

The body effects function in CapCut can enhance the appearance and movements of your subjects while adding a dynamic and eye-catching touch to your videos. This is the unprocessed video that we wish to add effects to.

In our practical, we will use two body effects. Use these procedures to apply and adjust body effects in CapCut:

Applying The Electric Storm Effect

CapCut's Electric Storm Effect delivers a striking visual enhancement by simulating a storm with lightning and electric currents. This effect adds drama and intensity to your video, boosting its visual appeal and making it more engaging for your audience.

To apply the Electric Storm effect, follow these steps:

1. Arrange the clips on the timeline and locate the section where you want to apply the effect.
2. Split the clip at the desired point and select the segment.
3. Access the effects menu and choose the *Body Effects* category with the clip selected.
4. Browse through the body effects and select the *Electric Storm* effect.

Once you've selected it, make some adjustments and preview the video to see if the effect is well applied.

The Light Dissolve Trending Effect

The Light Dissolve effect in CapCut is a visually striking transition that gradually brightens a video clip as it merges with another, creating a smooth and professional transition. This well-liked effect is ideal for giving your videos a smooth, professional look. Use these procedures to apply the Light Dissolve effect:

1. Open CapCut and import your video clips.
2. Arrange the clips on the timeline and select the section where you want to apply the effect.

3. Split the clip at the desired point and select the segment.
4. Navigate to the effects menu and choose the *Body Effects* option with the clip selected.
5. From the list of body effects, select the *Light Dissolve* effect.

APPLYING LIGHT DISSOLVE BODY EFFECTS ON CAPCUT MOBILE

Through the smooth blending of clips, CapCut's Light Dissolve effect provides a gentle, dreamlike transition that improves the visual flow of your video. To apply it on your mobile device via CapCut, take the following actions:

1. **Launch CapCut**: Open the project where you want to apply the Light Dissolve effect.

2. **Navigate to Effects**: To apply the effect, tap the clip you wish to use, and then tap the "Effects" button at the bottom of the screen.

3. **Locate Body Effects**: In the effects menu, select *Body Effects*.

4. **Find Trending**: Tap on the *Trending* tab and search for the Light Dissolve effect.

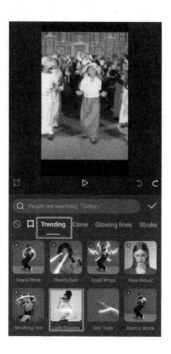

5. **Apply the Effect**: "Light Dissolve" can be found by searching or scrolling through Transitions or Trending. Apply the effect by tapping on it. Either the effect will be applied directly to the clip that was chosen, or it will produce a seamless transition between the two clips.

The Synergy of Transitions and Effects

When transitions and visual effects are used together, they amplify the storytelling and visual appeal of your content. Transitions provide structural flow, while visual effects add dynamism and creativity, ensuring your videos stand out in a competitive digital landscape. By mastering these techniques, you can produce videos that not only captivate but also leave a lasting impression on your audience.

AMAZING VIDEO FILTERS TO CREATE STUNNING VIDEOS

Do you require any artistic filters to alter the appearance of your video? Using one of the many different CapCut preset filters could give your film a whole new look. Free filters can be used to alter the theme, light, mood, color, and vibe. Feel free to use the filters you prefer to enhance the video and impress your audience.

Why Movie Filters Are Necessary

Filters are a vital part of filmmaking, offering both technical and artistic benefits that enhance visuals and deepen storytelling.

1. **Adjustment & Correction**: Filters are often used to correct imperfections in footage, such as fixing white balance, reducing glare, or compensating for uneven

lighting. These adjustments ensure the final product meets professional quality standards.

2. **Consistency**: Filters help maintain visual harmony across scenes shot in different locations or under varying lighting conditions. This ensures the film has a cohesive and unified aesthetic.

3. **Creative Storytelling**: Filters are an essential tool for conveying emotions and themes through visual elements, helping filmmakers shape how viewers perceive a scene.

4. **Enhancing Visual Appeal**: By adjusting elements like color, contrast, and brightness, filters enhance a scene's visual impact, creating a mood or atmosphere that aligns with the film's tone.

5. **Supporting the Narrative**: Filters are used to visually distinguish different parts of the story, such as indicating time shifts, changes in location, or emotional transitions.

6. **Visual Symbolism**: Filters can reinforce the underlying themes and ideas of a film, providing subtle yet meaningful layers to the visual storytelling.

How to Use CapCut Filters

1. Begin your project, and include your files.
2. Move your files to the Timeline.

3. Select the exact clip or clips you wish to add your filters.

4. Select the "Filter" option from the toolbar on the left, as seen earlier. Choose from a variety of filter effects by dropping the menu from the arrow visible on the filter.

5. Resize the filter to the desired time by adjusting its length.

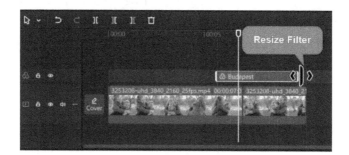

As shown in the screenshot below, I applied two filter effects—
The Life II from the Life category and *Oasis* from the Movie
Filters category—on a section of my video clip. Depending on
your desired outcome, you can further customize and
experiment with filters or other effects to showcase your
editing expertise and achieve a unique visual style.

Is there a clear difference between your original video and the
one you filtered? Using the same process, try experimenting
with adding additional filters to your movie.

APPLICATIONS FOR AMUSING STICKERS IN VIDEOS

CapCut offers a vast collection of editable stickers that can greatly improve your videos' aesthetic appeal and viewer engagement. These stickers are more than just ornaments; they are instruments to express your uniqueness, support the theme of your film, and make the viewing experience more engaging. The options are endless, regardless of whether you want to highlight particular aspects, add humor, or infuse your video with vitality.

Using CapCut's stickers is an excellent way to creatively express your ideas without incurring additional costs. By strategically placing stickers, you can highlight important moments, connect emotionally with your audience, and make your content more memorable. Beyond aesthetics, stickers also serve as a way to guide viewers' attention, making them an essential component of effective video storytelling.

Utilize all of CapCut's sticker collection to unleash your creative potential and produce videos that are impactful, professional, and entertaining.

Instructions for Adding Stickers to CapCut

Making your videos more visually appealing and interesting with CapCut may be as simple as adding stickers. To add stickers to your project, take the following actions:

1. Launch the app and open the project where you want to add stickers.
2. Tap on the video clip in the timeline where you'd like to place a sticker.
3. Tap the *Stickers* option to open CapCut's sticker library.
4. Browse through the available categories or search for a specific type of sticker that suits your video.
5. Tap on the desired sticker to add it to your clip. It will appear as an overlay on your video.
6. Drag the sticker to position it on the screen, and use pinch gestures to adjust its size.
7. Use the timeline to set how long the sticker will appear on the screen. Drag the edges of the sticker overlay to match the desired duration.

8. If needed, edit the sticker's properties, such as opacity, rotation, or animation effects, to fit your creative vision.

9. Play the clip to preview how the sticker appears in your video, and make adjustments as needed.

Changing the size of your sticker to suit your needs

The benefit of employing stickers in a video is that they can improve the visual appeal while efficiently conveying a certain message.

To resize illustrated stickers, start by placing your clip on the timeline and arranging it accordingly. Next, go to the top-left corner to find the stickers option within the media tools. Hover over the menu to the right and select the sticker you wish to use. After selecting, position the sticker where you want it on the clip.

CHAPTER 6

MEDIA ELEMENTS AND TRICKS

This chapter goes into great detail about advanced techniques for working with media assets in CapCut. Additionally, it gets you ready for the sophisticated editing methods that will be demonstrated. We will examine a few topics, including audio extraction from films, generic animation techniques, and text animation and advanced text. With these skills, you can create dynamic, engaging content and push the boundaries of your creativity.

What you'll learn:

- Increasing And Decreasing the Speed Of Video Clips
- Modifying Video Speed – Smartphone Guides
- CapCut Audio Extraction and Modification
- Working With Text and Titles
- How To Use the Timeline's Zoom-In-And-Out Feature

These and other sub-headings we shall be looking at in this Chapter. By the time we are through you should be much ready to start a professional project.

INCREASING AND DECREASING THE SPEED OF VIDEO CLIPS

CapCut's flexible speed modification tool allows users to swiftly and simply speed up or slow down their video clips. This tool is ideal for creating dynamic effects, emphasizing specific moments, and creating a slow-motion look.

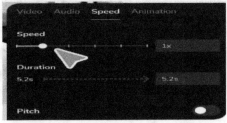

Benefits of the Speed Modification Feature in CapCut

- It helps improve storytelling by using slow-motion or fast-motion to emphasize key moments and enhance emotional impact.
- It increases visual appeal by adding dynamic effects that make your video more engaging and eye-catching.

- It offers creative flexibility, allowing you to experiment with different speeds to achieve unique looks and pacing for your content.
- It helps make your videos look polished and high-quality by giving you control over the speed of your clips.

Steps to Adjust the video's speed in CapCut: (Speed up and slow down)

1. Launch CapCut and get to your project.
2. Tap on the video clip in the timeline that you want to adjust, or apply the speed feature. It can be a section of the clip or all, depending on your workflow.
3. Tap on the *Speed* option at the Edit Pane of the screen, once your clip is selected.
4. Select either *Normal (Standard)* or *Curve*.

- *Normal* allows you to speed up or slow down the clip evenly.

- *Curve* gives you more control for custom speed changes at different points in the clip.

5. To speed up, drag the slider to the right. To slow down, drag the slider to the left.

6. Tap the play button to preview how the speed adjustment affects your clip.

7. Adjust the slider further as needed to get the desired effect.

8. Once you're satisfied with the speed adjustment, tap the checkmark to apply the changes.

CapCut also offers a speed curve. Following your selection of "Curve," many pre-made speed templates as well as a custom choice are displayed. You may adjust the semi-circle connection's speed from 0.1 to 10x by moving it up or down. To reverse the changes, click "Reset."

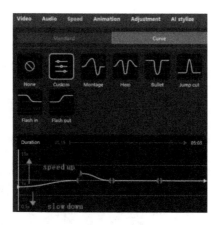

MODIFYING VIDEO SPEED – SMARTPHONE GUIDES

You can quickly adjust the video's tempo to your preferences with CapCut. Simply follow these steps on your phone to achieve this:

1. To begin, select a "New Project" or an already-existing project.

2. Import your video clip, make your adjustments, and select the clip to access the speed feature.

3. Click on the speed icon, to enable the settings and modify the features.

Follow the instructions you already saw above to adjust the settings to your delight.

Using CapCut's Speed Bar on Mobile

To slow down your video, swipe your finger left on the speed bar. Reducing the playback speed will extend the duration of your video. To increase the playback speed and create a fast-motion effect, swipe your finger to the right on the speed bar.

Follow the steps mentioned before to adjust the curve and modify the necessary features.

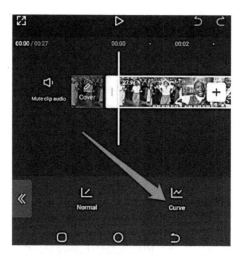

You can move the semi-circle connection up or down to change its speed from 0.1 to 10x. This works with templates as well. To undo the modifications, select "Reset."

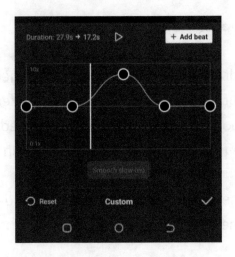

Adjust the playback speed of your video using the speed bar, which allows for a range from 0.1x to 100x. Play back your footage to preview and refine the changes until the speed meets your preferences. CapCut automatically saves your work, so you can easily return and make further adjustments if needed.

CAPCUT AUDIO EXTRACTION AND MODIFICATION

CapCut offers powerful tools for extracting and modifying audio, allowing you to take your video editing to the next level. With audio extraction, you can isolate soundtracks from video clips, enabling you to repurpose them or combine them with other media. The modification features let you fine-tune the extracted audio by adjusting volume, adding effects, trimming, or syncing it seamlessly with your visuals. These tools provide greater flexibility and creativity in crafting immersive, high-quality content.

Audio extraction from video is very easy and it can be used on both PCs and mobile devices. The following are the steps for each platform:

Audio Extraction Using CapCut PC:

1. Open the project containing the video clip in CapCut on your computer to extract the audio from it.
2. To incorporate the video clip into your project, select the file from your PC.
3. Place the film on the timeline.
4. Choose to extract the audio by doing a right-click on the video clip. Make sure that the audio and video clips are arranged in sync.

5. The audio clip will appear on the timeline underneath the video clip when you click to extract.

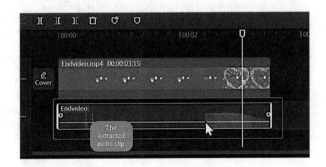

Audio Extraction Using CapCut Mobile:

1. Begin by importing your video clip into CapCut and arranging it on the timeline to organize your project.
2. Tap on the video clip you want to work with to select it and activate its editing options.
3. Navigate to the bottom menu, locate the audio extraction feature, and tap on it. This will separate the audio from the video, allowing you to edit or use the sound independently for creative purposes.

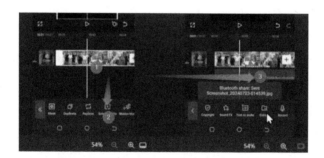

After completing the extraction, an audio clip icon with a waveform will appear directly beneath the video clip on the timeline. This visual representation allows for easy identification and editing of the extracted audio. More

140

advanced techniques for audio editing and customization will be explored in later sections. *[Your Honest review of this book will be much appreciated to help me fine-tune and advance the techniques employed in subsequent publications on this topic, so you can check back for updates on this guide. Thank you]*

WORKING WITH TEXT AND TITLES

Text and titles play a vital role in video editing, serving to enhance storytelling, provide context, and elevate the overall production quality of your content. They can guide viewers, emphasize key points, or add a creative flair to your videos. In this section, we will explore how to effectively add, edit, and customize text and titles using CapCut's versatile tools.

You will learn how to create basic text overlays for simplicity, add subtitles for clarity, and design dynamic, animated titles to grab attention. We'll also delve into advanced features like font customization, text effects, and timing synchronization to ensure your text integrates seamlessly with your visuals. By mastering CapCut's text capabilities, you can craft compelling narratives and produce visually appealing videos that resonate with your audience.

Advantages of Using Text and Titles in Media Editing Projects

- **Enhances Storytelling**: Text and titles help convey important messages, guiding viewers through the narrative and adding depth to the story.
- **Provides Context**: They deliver additional information, such as dates, locations, or speaker names, making content clearer and more informative.
- **Improves Accessibility**: Subtitles and captions make videos accessible to a broader audience, including those who are hearing-impaired or watching without sound.
- **Boosts Visual Appeal**: Creative fonts, styles, and animations add a professional touch and make the content more engaging.
- **Emphasizes Key Points**: Titles and text can highlight critical ideas or themes, ensuring they stand out to the viewer.
- **Aids Branding**: Consistent use of titles and text with specific fonts, colors, or logos reinforces brand identity.

142

- **Enhances Viewer Retention**: Dynamic and well-placed text elements can keep viewers engaged and focused throughout the video.
- **Facilitates Multilingual Content**: Text overlays allow for translations or subtitles, expanding the reach to international audiences.
- **Supports Instructional Content**: Text is crucial for tutorials or educational videos, providing step-by-step instructions or highlighting important points.

Instructions for Including Text in Your Video:

1. Open CapCut on your mobile device to begin editing your video.
2. Browse your media library and select a video clip that you want to work with, starting a new project.
3. In the top-left corner of the screen, tap on the *Text* tool. This will open the text editing menu, allowing you to add and customize text for your video.
4. Tap "Add Text" to add new text. After determining the precise location of your text on your video clip, you may also press on the Default Text (+). A text box will appear in the preview window of your movie.

5. To make changes, tap the text box and use the edit window to type the text you wish to write.

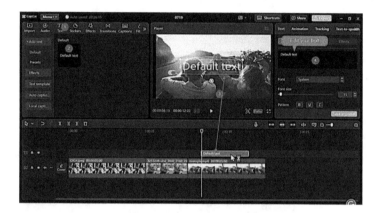

Let's say we're documenting a tour and want to share with our audience how far we've traveled or how long we've been on the road. We can use text to highlight this information effectively. In this section, we'll walk through the process of adding that text practically.

First, let's go back and revise the default text we added earlier, picking up from where we left off. This will allow us to tailor the message and make it more relevant to the current part of the video.

1. Put the following in uppercase: "We've traveled 460 kilometers as of noon! What a fantastic adventure." Go ahead and select your desired font features.
2. Preview your video and apply any needed changes.

Applying Text Effects, and Styles to your video:

Choosing the right font style is crucial for ensuring that your video effectively communicates its message while also being visually appealing. The font you select should complement the tone and theme of the content, making it easier for your audience to read and understand. A well-chosen font enhances the overall viewer experience, creating a harmonious balance between design and message, while reinforcing the emotional impact of the video.

In this section, we will use our earlier work to demonstrate how to choose and use several font styles in CapCut. To create text pieces that both precisely match the overall concept of your video and enhance its visual appeal, you will learn how to select a font, alter font sizes, add effects, position text, and apply colors.

Working With Font Face:

The final appearance and feel of your film can be significantly impacted by your choice of font face in CapCut. To choose and change the font face in CapCut, follow these steps:

146

1. Tap the "Text" option in the upper-left corner of the screen.
2. Select "Default Text" to add a new text layer, or choose an existing text layer to modify.
3. Once the text layer is selected, modification options will appear in the right pane.
4. Tap "Font" to browse through the available typefaces.

CapCut offers a variety of font styles, including serif, sans-serif, ornamental, and handwritten fonts.

Working with Text Effects and Animations in CapCut

You may improve the visual impact of your material with CapCut's variety of text effects and animations, which will draw readers in and make your text stand out. An alphabetical summary of the available text effects and animation choices is provided here:

Text Effects:

- **Glow**: Apply a glowing aura around your text to make it more eye-catching. You can adjust both the color and intensity of the glow to fit the desired effect for your video.
- **Opacity**: Control the transparency of your text, allowing you to make it fully visible or more subtle, blending with the background or emphasizing the text as needed.
- **Outline**: Add a border around your text to ensure it stands out, especially against complex or busy backgrounds. You can customize the outline's thickness and color for a tailored effect.
- **Shadow**: Create a shadow effect behind your text to give it depth and a more three-dimensional appearance. Customize the shadow's color, opacity, distance, and angle to fine-tune its look.

Text Animations:

- **3D Text Effects**: Some CapCut versions allow you to apply 3D text effects, which give your text a sense of perspective and depth, making it appear as though it's emerging from the screen.

- **In and Out Animations**: Add animations to text as it enters and exits the screen. Popular animations like fade, slide, zoom, and bounce can be used to create fluid, engaging transitions.

- **Kinetic Typography**: Use preset kinetic typography to animate your text in sync with music or narration, creating a dynamic, rhythm-based experience for the viewer.

- **Loop Animations**: Keep your text moving continuously throughout the video with looped animations. This technique adds vibrancy and maintains viewer interest.

- **Text Masking**: Reveal your text behind shapes or objects with a masking effect. This creative animation technique works well for smooth transitions or adding a unique artistic flair.

- **Color Gradients**: Apply multi-color gradients to your text for a visually striking effect. You can adjust the gradient's colors and direction to fit the overall style and tone of your video.

- **Textures and Patterns**: Enhance your text with various textures or patterns, giving it a distinctive look that stands out and adds extra visual appeal.

The quality of your film can be greatly improved by skillfully utilizing these text effects and animations, which will make the text more dynamic and captivating while also matching your overall creative concept.

Here's how to use CapCut's Text Effects feature:

1. Click the Text Feature and, and quickly move to the Effect option.
2. Select the Effect you want to apply.
3. While the Textbox is still active, you can change the text's appearance from the edit pane to suit your tastes.

4. Do some adjustments to make sure the glow effect looks the way you want it to, and preview your video.

Adding Animations to Text

Using CapCut to add dynamic and compelling animations to text elements could enhance your film's visual appeal. You may use and alter animations to manage how text appears, moves, or disappears to draw attention to key spots and give your content a polished look. Following these steps can help you apply Animation to Text:

1. Begin by creating a new project in CapCut.

2. Select "Text" to include a text layer in your project. Customize the text by adjusting the font, size, and color to suit your preferences. You can also apply any previously created effects if desired.

3. Tap on the text clip in the timeline to select it, then modify the text duration or length to fit your needs.

4. Choose the "Animation" button, and select either the "In," "Out," or "Loop" animation depending on how you want the text to appear and move.

5. Fine-tune the animation by adjusting its duration, speed, and style to achieve the desired effect.

6. To view how the text animation looks and make any necessary adjustments, play your project.

Video Adjustments: Contrast, Saturation, Brightness, and Color

In this section, we'll explore essential video adjustments such as contrast, saturation, brightness, and color. These tools are fundamental in refining the visual aesthetics of your footage, enabling you to create more engaging and professional-looking videos.

Why Adjustments Are Important

The ability to adjust the visual elements of your video is crucial in video editing. These adjustments help enhance the overall look and feel of your footage, making it more appealing to your audience. Whether you're working on a personal project, professional film, or social media post, fine-tuning your video can significantly improve its impact.

How to Fine-Tune Your Video's Appearance
Here is some key video adjustments you can make:

- **Brightness**: Adjust the brightness to lighten or darken your video, ensuring the proper exposure for your scenes.

- **Contrast**: Modify contrast to highlight the differences between light and dark areas, creating a more dynamic and visually striking image.
- **Exposure**: Adjust the exposure to correct footage that is either overexposed (too bright) or underexposed (too dark), ensuring even lighting throughout your video.
- **Sharpen**: Use sharpening to improve the clarity and detail in your video, giving it a crisper, more defined appearance.
- **Saturation**: Control the saturation to adjust the intensity of colors in your video. Increasing saturation makes the colors more vivid while decreasing it can create a more muted effect.
- **Temperature**: Adjust the color temperature to set the overall tone of your video, making it warmer (yellow/orange tones) or cooler (blue tones) depending on the mood you want to convey.
- **Vignette**: Apply a vignette effect to darken the edges of your video, focusing attention on the center of the frame and emphasizing key subjects.

By mastering these video adjustments, you can significantly enhance the visual quality of your content, ensuring it matches the desired mood and resonates with your audience.

Now that you have a better grasp of these elements, let's go through the steps to apply them.

1. Start by creating a new project by tapping the "New Project" button.
2. Import your video clips and arrange them on the timeline.
3. Trim and select the part of the video you want to adjust, which will activate the edit pane.
4. Tap the "**Adjustment**" tab to access various settings and fine-tune elements like brightness, contrast, saturation, and more.

Examine your video and make any necessary edits. Go through the "Basic," "HSL," and "Curve" options.

Video Clips with In-and-Out Animation

When used in video editing, animations can give your content a polished, dynamic appearance that will grab and hold viewers' attention. One of the most effective techniques is to use in-and-out animations, which add transition or movement effects to the start (in) and finish (out) of video segments.

Why Use Animation in Videos?

Incorporating animations into your videos can significantly enhance their visual appeal and audience engagement. Animations are particularly effective for introducing or concluding scenes, providing a seamless and professional touch. This section will explore the different types of animations available, demonstrate how to integrate in-and-out animations into video clips, and share techniques for maximizing their impact on your content.

Applying the In-and-Out Animations in CapCut

These steps will guide you through adding animations to your videos:

1. Import your video clips into your video editing application to animate them. Select the clip of the video that you want to animate.
2. Navigate to the "Animation" section for animations, once you've decided the section of clips to include them.

3. Select the animation effect you want to use to begin your clip. Zoom-in, slide-in, and fade-in are popular choices. Variables like duration and direction can be changed to achieve the desired effect.

4. Similarly, choose an animation effect for the end of your clip. Some helpful alternatives are fade out, slide out, and spin out. Adapt the settings to the style of your video.

To see how the animations look, watch the preview of the clip. Make any necessary adjustments to ensure that the animations are visually appealing. Before exporting the video in the format of your choosing, ensure that the animations are rendered appropriately.

HOW TO USE THE TIMELINE'S ZOOM-IN-AND-OUT FEATURE

The timeline's zoom-in-and-out functionality is an essential tool for effective video editing. It improves your creative workflow and enables you to precisely manage your project.

Why It's Important to Regularly Utilize the Feature:
- **Precise Editing**: Zooming in lets you make detailed adjustments, ensuring smoother clip transitions and accurate edits.

- **Error Detection**: Close-up views help spot and correct minor mistakes that might be overlooked otherwise.
- **Efficient Organization**: Zooming out provides a holistic view of your project, making it easier to structure scenes and maintain a cohesive flow.
- **Enhanced Creativity**: The ability to switch perspectives fosters flexibility, enabling you to experiment with new ideas and refine your work.

Steps to Apply the Zoom Control Features:

When attempting to zoom in or out, you have two options: Use the timeline's Zoom tool. Alternatively, if you're a Mac user, you can swiftly use Cmd + Mouse Wheel; if you're a Windows user, you may use Ctrl + Mouse Wheel.

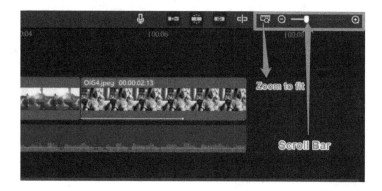

CHAPTER 7

WORKING ON AUDIO AND SOUND IN CAPCUT

Audio plays a critical role in creating engaging and professional video content, and CapCut offers a comprehensive suite of tools for audio editing. Whether you're a beginner or an experienced user, this chapter provides an in-depth guide to the key features and processes involved in enhancing your project's sound quality.

From basic adjustments to advanced techniques, you'll learn how to make the most of CapCut's audio capabilities to elevate your videos.

What you will learn in this Chapter:

- What is Audio in Video Editing?
- Main Audio Sources in CapCut.
- Using CapCut's Voice Changer Feature to Improve Your Voice
- Including Background Music in CapCut

WHAT IS AUDIO IN VIDEO EDITING?

In video editing, **audio** refers to all sound elements integrated into a video project, including dialogue, music, sound effects, and ambient noise. It plays a vital role in shaping the viewer's experience, enhancing storytelling, and setting the tone or mood of the content. Effective use of audio requires syncing it with images, adjusting levels for clarity and balance, and using effects to create a polished and immersive end product. It's a crucial component that guarantees the message and emotions of a video are successfully delivered.

MAIN AUDIO SOURCES IN CAPCUT:

CapCut provides users with multiple options for importing and producing audio, making it versatile for various creative needs. Whether you're using the desktop or mobile version, the process is straightforward and user-friendly. Below are the main sources for adding audio in CapCut:

1. **CapCut Audio Library:**
2. **Importing Audio from Your Device**
3. **Recording Audio Directly in CapCut**
4. **Text-to-Speech**

CapCut lets you make videos with excellent sound that accentuates your images by utilizing these three audio sources.

Method 1: Using CapCut Audio Library

CapCut features a built-in library of music, sound effects, and audio clips. This extensive collection of royalty-free audio options allows you to easily find sounds that match the tone and style of your video, saving you time and ensuring professional results.

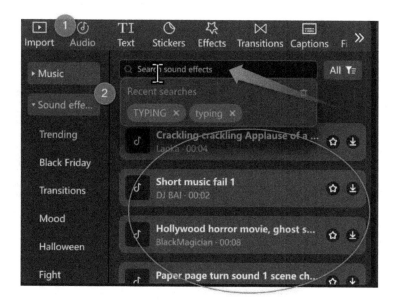

Steps to do this:

1. Start a new project or on your existing project.
2. Move to the Audio Section in the Menu
3. Browse or search for music by genre or mood.
4. Click the plus icon once you have downloaded and previewed the music to add it to your timeline.

Once these steps are carried out, you will find the video clip on the timeline where you pointed to locate it. CapCut also allows you the features to edit or adjust the sound once downloaded.

Method 2: Importing Audio from Your Device: You can upload custom audio files directly from your computer or mobile device. This option is ideal for using personal recordings, external sound effects, or licensed tracks, offering complete creative flexibility.

Steps to do this:

1. Click Import to upload an audio file.
2. Choose the desired audio file from your device's storage.
3. Your media library will display the audio file once it has been uploaded.
4. Now you have the Audio file at hand. Drag it to the timeline to continue your work.

Note: Verify that the audio clip is precisely where you want it to start. Therefore, after you move it to the timeline, you can change its size and position.

Method 3: Recording Audio Directly in CapCut: CapCut also allows users to record audio directly within the app. This is particularly useful for adding voiceovers or capturing on-the-spot sound, ensuring a seamless integration of original audio content into your project.

How to use CapCut to record audio:

1. Drag your video clip to the timeline after importing it.
2. Put the videos in the right order on the timeline.
3. The voice recording tool is located directly above the timeline. Click on it, choose to cut down on echoes, and then set the level to your preference.

4. Once you click you should see a screen like this.

5. Press the record button.

When you're finished, align the audio and video clips, and attempt to improve your clip using the audio or sound modification we previously utilized.

USING CAPCUT'S VOICE CHANGER FEATURE TO IMPROVE YOUR VOICE:

Having top-notch audio when editing videos can significantly boost the overall impact of your work. CapCut's versatile voice changer feature makes it simple to edit and enhance your audio recordings. Whether using a PC or a mobile device, CapCut is a feature that adds a range of audio effects to your films. Other functions like speech-to-song and voice filter and character are available under the voice changer. These effects can provide drama, humor, or uniqueness. To ensure that your audio is clear and perfectly aligned with your visual content, this section will explain how to use CapCut's voice changer tool. Get ready to develop your video editing skills by altering your audio, from basic voiceovers to complex adjustments.

Key Considerations Before Enhancing or Modifying Voice in Video Editing

Improving or changing voice in video editing can have a big impact on the project's impact and overall quality. A careful approach is necessary to get professional results, regardless of your goal—whether it is to increase clarity, apply creative effects, or guarantee tonal consistency.

This section outlines important things to think about from the very beginning of the recording process to the very end of the editing process to make sure your voiceovers provide value to your video. These widely accepted best practices are essential to efficiently producing media.

Things to observe During this process:
Audience and Purpose:

- **Understand Your Target Audience**: Tailor voice modifications to align with the preferences and needs of your intended viewers.
- **Align with Video Goals**: Ensure voice enhancements support the video's purpose—whether to inform, entertain, or persuade.

Recording Quality
- **Choose a Quiet Environment**: Record in a calm setting to minimize background noise.
- **Use a High-Quality Microphone**: Invest in a good microphone to ensure clear and rich sound.
- **Utilize a Pop Filter**: Reduce plosive sounds like "p" and "b" for smoother audio.
- **Maintain Proper Microphone Distance**: Position yourself at an appropriate distance to avoid distortion and achieve balanced sound quality.

Voice Modification and Effects

- **Noise Reduction**: Apply noise reduction tools to eliminate unwanted background sounds without sacrificing vocal clarity.

- **Equalization (EQ)**: Adjust frequencies to enhance vocal warmth, richness, and distinction.
- **Compression**: Balance loud and soft sections to improve overall volume consistency and professionalism.

Synchronization (When Applicable)

- **Lip Sync Accuracy**: For videos featuring visible speakers, ensure the voice matches their lip movements.
- **Timing Precision**: Align audio with visual elements to create a seamless and natural flow.

Legal and Ethical Considerations

- **Obtain Necessary Permissions**: If modifying someone else's voice, ensure you have explicit approval to do so.
- **Respect Representation**: Be mindful of how voice alterations might impact the speaker's image or message.

How to Improve Your Audio Clip:

1. Choose between beginning a new project or selecting an already existing one.
2. Upload your images or videos.
3. Sort and move your media to the timeline.
4. To begin recording, locate the microphone icon and click.

5. When the countdown is over, speak loudly into the microphone. When the recording is complete, click to end it.
6. As needed, split, edit, or cut recorded audio.

To open the Edit window, select the audio clip, then work on improving your voice.

Listen to the audio recording of your project again to make sure it enhances the other material. Any necessary timing or audio modifications should be made.

Method 4: Create an Audio Using Text-to-Speech System

Adding voice narration to your flicks will make them much more approachable and captivating. Additionally, this will enhance the narrative experience. CapCut's convenient Text-to-Speech (TTS) feature allows you to convert written text into spoken sentences. Whether using a PC or a mobile device, this function could save you time and effort by automating voiceovers. By using the advice given here, you may be certain that your films sound clear and polished.

Text-to-Speech: What is it?

Text-to-speech technology uses software to analyze written text and produce a voice that sounds human to read it out. Due to its effectiveness, accessibility, and convenience, TTS systems are widely utilized in a wide range of devices and applications. The following are some crucial TTS facts:

Key Features of Text-to-Speech (TTS) Technology

Text-to-speech (TTS) systems offer a range of versatile features, making them valuable tools across various applications. Below are the key features, organized for clarity and progression:

- **Accessibility**: TTS technology provides an audio version of written content, making it indispensable for individuals with visual impairments or reading difficulties.

- **Language Support**: Many TTS systems support multiple languages, enabling use in global and multilingual contexts.
- **Voice Selection**: Users can choose from a variety of voices, including different genders, accents, and tones, to suit their specific needs.
- **Customization**: TTS enables users to customize the output to their liking by allowing them to alter speech characteristics like volume, pitch, and speed.
- **Integration**: To improve usefulness and convenience, TTS can easily interface with a variety of hardware and software, including PCs, e-readers, cellphones, and virtual assistants.

Benefits of Text-to-Speech

Text-to-speech (TTS) technology provides several advantages, including **time efficiency**, as it rapidly transforms extensive text into audio, streamlining tasks. It ensures **uniformity** by offering a consistent voice and tone, ideal for professional use and brand representation. Moreover, its **flexibility** makes it compatible with various platforms and devices, catering to diverse applications.

Procedure for Using Text-to-Speech:

The process of creating text-to-speech (TTS) audio is easy with CapCut. Here's how to do it on both a PC and a mobile device:

1. **Add Text**: Click on the "Add Text" option and enter the text you wish to convert to speech.
2. **Select TTS**: In the text editing toolbar, click the "TTS" (Text-to-Speech) button.
3. **Choose Language and Voice**: Select the desired language and voice style for the speech output.
4. **Adjust Parameters**: Customize settings such as pitch, speed, or volume if necessary.

1. **Generate Audio**: Click "Generate" to create the TTS audio.

2. **Place on Timeline**: The generated audio will automatically appear on your timeline, ready for use.

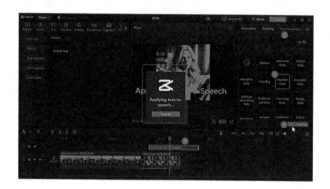

As needed, move, crop, and alter the audio on the timeline. After you're finished, preview your work and remove the text clips.

To utilize the Text-to-Speech feature on mobile in CapCut, start by launching the app, creating a new project, and importing your media onto the timeline. Tap the "Text" icon at the bottom of the screen, select "Text to Audio," and enter your desired text. After confirming by clicking "Done," choose a voice from the available options or record your own for a personalized touch. Allow the text-to-speech tool to process and generate the audio, then remove the text clip and focus on the generated audio clip. Finally, preview your video, and if necessary, enhance the audio clarity by adjusting the volume using the "Volume" option. This ensures your voiceover is clear and perfectly suited to your project.

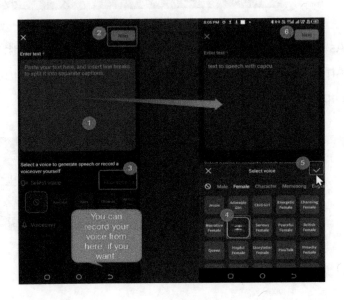

Once you are ready to download your work, remember to remove the text snippets that were utilized to create the audio.

INCLUDING BACKGROUND MUSIC IN CAPCUT

Users can choose from a wide variety of background music options included with CapCut to go with their video tales. You can also import your favorite tracks straight from your device, as previously mentioned. We should add the background music and modify it for our video.

How to Add and Adjust Background Music in CapCut:

1. Open CapCut and import the desired audio for background music.
2. Drag and drop the audio clip onto the timeline.
3. Position the audio clip accurately on the timeline.

4. Adjust the audio volume to match the video's sound balance.

> Navigate to the "Settings" or "Edit Window" on the right pane.

> Click the "Basic" button to increase or decrease the volume.

5. Preview the video to ensure the background music is playing correctly.

CHAPTER 8

POPULAR VIDEO EDITING TECHNIQUES IN CAPCUT

New capabilities and artistic effects that improve video footage are highlighted in recent advancements in CapCut video editing techniques. This Chapter discusses a few of the most often-used methods at the moment.

What you will learn:

- CapCut overlay techniques
- The CapCut's critical green screen/chroma techniques
- Motion tracking in CapCut
- Working with keyframe in CapCut
- CapCut's auto-captioning
- Adding body effects to videos

CAPCUT OVERLAY TECHNIQUES

One of the most powerful advantages of CapCut overlays is the ability to blend and stack several overlays. You can create complex, multi-layered effects with this, which can enhance the overall look and feel of your videos. Applying overlays in the right order is important because it can significantly impact the final product. Layering a text overlay over a visual overlay could help make the text easier to read. You can blend overlays by changing their opacities and blending modes. This can help you create unique visual distortions, dimension and depth, and seamless transitions. CapCut's overlays are amazing tools that let you embellish your videos with effects, stickers, logos, and more. Professionals often use this feature for editing.

CapCut Overlays: What Are They?

You can superimpose one element on top of another in a picture or video by using CapCut overlays. It is possible to include text, logos, and more images or movies in the same frame. Unlike other programs like In-Shot or Filmora, where you usually have to pay for this function, CapCut offers these for free, which is why it's so great. In contrast to CapCut, the main feature of both programs' premium versions is overlays.

Benefits of Using Overlays in CapCut

- Overlays allow you to add multiple elements like text, images, stickers, and logos on top of your video, enabling you to create more visually engaging content.
- The ability to layer various elements gives you greater creative control, allowing for intricate designs and unique video compositions.
- You can combine different overlays, such as text on images or video, to create more complex, dynamic visuals.
- CapCut offers blending modes and opacity settings to modify how overlays interact with the video, allowing you to achieve smooth transitions, distortion effects, and depth.
- Unlike many other video editing apps, CapCut offers overlays for free, making it an attractive option for content creators who want professional-level effects without paying extra.
- The overlay feature is user-friendly, requiring minimal effort to drag and place elements, which is ideal for beginners and professionals alike.

Let's get down to business and discuss several popular overlays in CapCut. This part will provide you with a step-by-step tutorial on how to apply various overlays to CapCut.

Instructions for Adding Text Overlay to a Video:

1. Launch CapCut, then tap "New Project."
2. Select your video and drag it onto the timeline.
3. Tap the Text icon, then select "Default Text." Enter your text and customize the font, size, color, and location.
4. Move the text to your desired location. Adjust the duration by sliding the text layer's borders in the timeline.
5. Preview to see your work.

How to Add a Video Overlay to a Video:

Stepp1: Start a new project.

At the top, click the "Create Project" button. Click Import to add your videos.

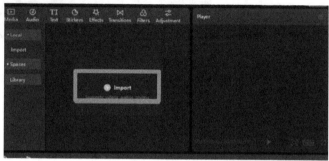

Step 2: Include a video overlay.

Click the addition sign "+" to add the movie to the timeline and choose which one to use as the background.

To ensure that both videos are playing simultaneously, drag and drop the video you want to overlay onto the timeline. Drag the video upward after selecting it to use as an overlay. There will be new video footage as a result.

To change the size of the overlay, you may also utilize the Scale tool on the right. Additionally, by browsing the video player area and moving the points in each corner, you may reposition the overlay within the frame of the player window.

Step 3: You can preview and export your video:

To check if the video meets your expectations, play it quickly using the preview button. Share your video after exporting it.

THE CRITICAL GREEN SCREEN/CHROMA TECHNIQUES

The green screen method, sometimes referred to as chroma key, is used in video production to change the color of a solid background—typically green—or overlay various video segments. This method seamlessly blends several segments to produce more inventive and dynamic videos using CapCut.

With the use of green screen technology, filmmakers can create immersive environments for narrating adventure stories, showcasing products in intriguing surroundings, or capturing stunning outdoor scenes. With the use of green screen technology, filmmakers can create immersive environments for narrating adventure stories, showcasing products in intriguing surroundings, or capturing stunning outdoor scenes.

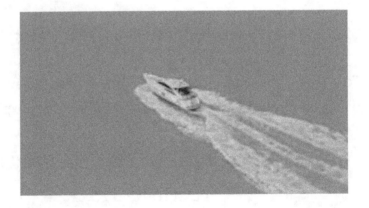

By using green screen or chroma key techniques, you can significantly enhance your CapCut video editing abilities. Using green screen or chroma key techniques can significantly improve your CapCut video editing skills. Here are several reasons why this feature is valuable:

- **Consistency**: Green screen technology ensures consistent lighting and backgrounds across different scenes or takes, creating a uniform look throughout your video.
- **Creative Flexibility**: With a green screen, you can place almost any image or video as the background, giving you endless creative options that would be limited in real-world settings.
- **Efficiency**: By eliminating the need for location shots or complex set designs, green screen editing saves both time and money, especially for smaller productions or independent creators.
- **Enhanced Visual Appeal**: Removing background clutter can make your video cleaner and more visually appealing, which is essential for capturing and maintaining viewers' attention.
- **Professional Look**: A green screen allows you to remove distracting elements and focus on the subject, giving your video a more polished and professional appearance.

- **User-Friendly**: CapCut's green screen tool is simple to use, allowing you to easily replace the green background with any other image or video, helping to elevate the quality and creativity of your content.
- **Versatility**: Whether you're creating tutorials, product demos, or storytelling videos, the green screen enables you to place your subject in any scenario or environment without the need for physical presence.

Remove the Green Screen with the Chroma Key

CapCut's Chroma Key feature lets you replace a green or blue screen with any image or video, making it easy to change backgrounds and create dynamic effects. By selecting and removing a specific color, you can overlay new backgrounds, making your subject appear in entirely different settings. It's a versatile tool for enhancing creativity, adding special effects, and elevating your video content.

Steps to do this:
1. On your PC or mobile device, launch the CapCut app, then tap the "New Project" icon.
2. Import and move the image or video that you want to use as the background to the timeline.

3. Import your green screen clip into CapCut, then position it over the original video or image to create an overlay on the timeline.

4. Adjust the size and angle of the green screen clip to fit your desired layout over the background video.

5. To activate the **chroma key** feature, click the **Remove BG** button in the Editing Pane, choose the Chroma Key option, and then use the picker tool to select the green color as seen here.

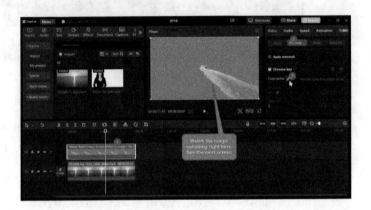

6. Hover your mouse pointer over the green screen to select the green color after turning on the chroma feature. By doing this, the green background will be eliminated, revealing the main video's background underneath.

7. To successfully remove any remaining green, adjust the background's shadow and intensity after removing it.

8. Adjust the object's size to your preference and place it correctly. Applying transitional or filter

effects might assist in highlighting a realistic concept.

9. To make sure your work is flawless, play it before exporting it.

MOTION TRACKING IN CAPCUT

With CapCut, you may use the motion-tracking capability to add text, stickers, or other elements to moving objects in your movie. The video's energy and engagement are enhanced by this technique. CapCut uses tracking points to assess and follow the object's motion, ensuring that the extra piece moves in sync with the object. Using this feature to add remarks, subtitles, or graphics that follow moving subjects can make your video edits look more professional.

Applications for Motion Tracking:

- Education Films: Motion tracking keeps viewers focused on key elements in tutorials, such as following an artist's drawing or a teacher experimenting.
- Filmmaking: Used to seamlessly integrate CGI elements with live-action, such as applying digital effects like scars or makeup that move naturally with the actor.
- Interactive Presentations: Ensures text or images stay aligned with a moving presenter, making presentations engaging and easier to follow.

- Music Videos: Tracks performers or dancers to add text, animations, or effects that move in sync, enhancing visual appeal.
- Product Demonstrations: Highlights features of rotating or moving products by aligning descriptions, labels, or prices with them.
- Sports Analysis: Tracks players or the ball to provide real-time stats or visuals, drawing attention to key elements in the game.
- Vlogs and Travel Videos: Adds moving text labels to landmarks, making the content more informative and engaging.

Practice with Motion Tracking Techniques

This is a detailed tutorial on how to use CapCut for motion-tracking exercises. Our goal is to partially monitor the speed boat's movement:

1. To begin editing in CapCut, launch the app and start a new project. Import your video clip onto the timeline and arrange your clips in the desired order for seamless storytelling or flow.

2. Choose the video clip on your timeline, then tap the "Tracking" option from the menu. A small square will appear on the video; place it accurately over the object or area you wish to track.

3. Add a tracking element to your video, such as a location sticker for this example. Place the tracking points on a specific part of your video. Choose the tracking direction—either forward or backward. In this case, select forward motion.

After selecting "Start," watch for the process to finish. Adjust the size and location of the tracking points to ensure they cover the features you want to track.

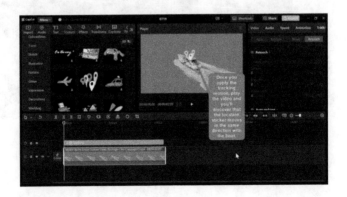

Note: CapCut will monitor the tracking points and evaluate movement during the video clip. To ensure that the tracking points are appropriately followed, monitor the development.

WORKING WITH KEYFRAME IN CAPCUT

Keyframes are essential for creating smooth, dynamic animations in CapCut. They allow you to control changes over time, such as moving an object, adjusting its size, or modifying its opacity. To use keyframes, place them on the timeline at points where you want specific changes to start and end. For instance, you can make text move across the screen or gradually zoom in on a video clip. By adding multiple keyframes, you can achieve complex effects, ensuring transitions and animations look seamless. This tool is highly versatile, making it a favorite for both beginners and professional editors.

How helpful is Keyframe in Multimedia?

In multimedia creation, keyframes are immensely useful since they allow for exact control over effects, animations, and transitions. This is why they are essential:

- **Smooth Transitions**: Keyframes allow for gradual changes, such as fading audio, zooming, or panning, which makes multimedia content visually appealing and professional.
- **Customization**: They give creators the ability to fine-tune movements, making animations and effects uniquely tailored to the project's needs.
- **Storytelling Enhancement**: Keyframes can guide a viewer's focus, highlight key details, or create dynamic sequences, improving the narrative flow.
- **Efficiency**: By defining starting and ending points, keyframes automate transitions, reducing the need for frame-by-frame adjustments.
- **Creative Flexibility**: From simple animations to complex motion graphics, keyframes allow for limitless creativity across various media types, including videos, presentations, and interactive content.

How to use Keyframe in CapCut to create a zoom effect:

Use CapCut's keyframes to create a smooth zoom effect by doing the following:

1. Bring your media clip into the timeline by importing it.
2. To apply the keyframe effect, arrange your clips and trim them at the precise point.
3. Choose the video clip to which you want to apply the keyframe.
4. Place the playhead where you want the zoom effect to begin on the footage.
5. Locate the keyframe icon (often a diamond shape) and tap it to create your first keyframe. This shows the beginning of your Zoom.

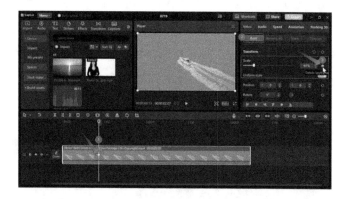

6. Place the playhead in the desired location for the second keyframe. Change the scale of the

movie, zoom in or out. This change will automatically create the second keyframe.

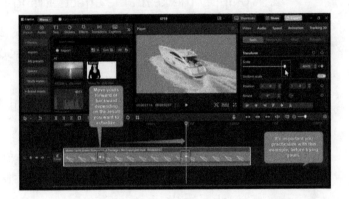

Have you noticed anything? As we look at the object of attention, our video clip on the preview screen gets larger. If the zoom alters the framing of your topic, you may need to adjust the position of the clip. Make sure the focal point remains in the desired area of the frame.

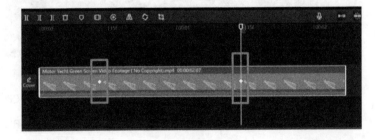

To see the smooth zoom effect, watch the video. CapCut will interpolate the frames between the two keyframes to provide a seamless transition. The zoom effect can be made faster or slower by changing the keyframes to alter the time.

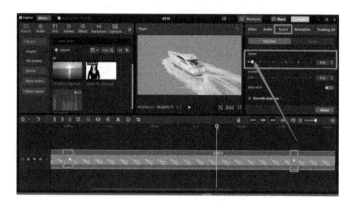

CAPCUT'S AUTO-CAPTIONING

Subtitles are vital for making videos accessible to diverse audiences, including multilingual viewers and those with hearing impairments. Manually creating subtitles can be time-intensive and complex, but CapCut's AI-powered auto-captioning streamlines the process. This tool benefits content creators, marketers, and viewers alike by quickly generating accurate subtitles and enhancing accessibility and user engagement.

A Comprehensive Guide to Auto Caption Generation

1. Launch the CapCut app on your PC or mobile device. You can either tap on an existing project to add captions, or you can tap on "New Project" to start a new one. Add the video you want to modify to your project timeline after selecting it from your file system or gallery.

2. Locate and tap the "Text" item on the toolbar. Find the "Auto Caption" option (it may also be called "Auto Subtitles" or "Auto-Generate Captions") and select it. This technology will automatically generate captions for the spoken information in your video.

3. After selecting the "4" generate button, wait. CapCut is going to supply captions. How long this takes may depend on how long the video is.

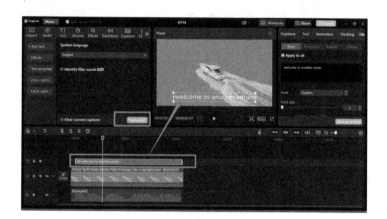

4. Verify the generated captions to ensure they are correct. You can correct any errors or off-time times so that the audio and captions are perfectly synced.
5. Change the font style, size, color, and placement of the captions to make the text easier to read and to match the look of your movie. After making all the necessary adjustments, save your work and export the video with captions. Choose the desired resolution and format for your final video.

ADDING BODY EFFECTS TO VIDEOS

Lightening Eyes Effect in CapCut

The Lightning Eyes Effect from CapCut is a powerful and dynamic effect that gives the appearance of electrical energy or lightning bouncing from the eyes. It is well-known for creating dramatic, colorful visuals, especially for action-packed or supernaturally themed projects, and it is located in CapCut's Body Effects category. When combined with other effects, this effect can create more complex visual narratives and is a great way to add a dramatic or eerie feel to your videos. The steps to activate the effect are as follows:

1. Add your video clip to the media pane.
2. Transfer it to the Timeline, then pick the clip to which you wish to apply an effect.
3. Under Effects, select Body Effects. Then, pick and use the Lightning Eyes effect.

4. As necessary, change the settings. Save or export your video after previewing it.

Apply Flipped Background Effect

Let's demonstrate how to use CapCut's Flipped Background effect, which will help you add a stylish, modern appearance to your videos. Whether you want to experiment with different visual styles or create a dreamy appearance, this effect is a great way to add some originality to your content. The steps to apply the effect are as follows:

1. Just like the steps followed above in adding the Eye-lightening Effect, Arrange your clips.
2. Select the exact clip in the timeline to apply the effects.
3. Locate the Body Effects under Effects, then choose Background.
4. Select the Flipped effect and apply it.

After previewing your film and making any necessary settings changes, save or export it.

CONCLUSION

This book has provided an in-depth exploration of CapCut, from its core features to advanced techniques, empowering you to take full control of your video editing projects. Whether you're a beginner or an experienced creator, CapCut offers a wealth of tools that can elevate your content creation process.

We began by exploring the fundamentals of CapCut, such as understanding the **timeline**, **clips**, and **layers**. Mastering these basics allows you to organize and structure your video efficiently. With the **Trim**, **Split**, and **Crop** tools, you can refine your footage to perfection, ensuring that only the best parts make it into your final product.

As you grow more comfortable with these basic tools, you can dive into **advanced features** like **Chroma Key**, **Masking**, and **Blend Modes**. These techniques open up new possibilities, allowing you to replace backgrounds, add visual effects, and create seamless transitions between scenes. Tools like **Keyframes**, **Speed Curves**, and **Text-to-Speech** give you the ability to animate elements, control timing, and add engaging voiceovers, helping to bring your vision to life in dynamic and creative ways.

210

We also covered essential **audio editing tools** like **Volume Envelopes**, **Audio Tracks**, and **Waveforms**. Whether you're adjusting sound levels, syncing audio with visuals, or adding background music, these tools are vital for enhancing the mood and atmosphere of your video.

Throughout the chapters, we emphasized the importance of understanding **visual effects**, such as **Filters**, **LUTs (Look-Up Tables)**, and **Mosaic Effects**. These effects help you control the aesthetics of your video, setting the tone and style to suit your creative direction. Additionally, CapCut's **Stickers**, **Custom Stickers**, and **Text Styles** offer endless possibilities for adding creative elements that enhance the visual appeal and engagement of your content.

As you've learned, CapCut's wide array of features—from simple edits to intricate effects—makes it a versatile and powerful tool for all types of videos projects. The book provides a **step-by-step guide** to understanding and mastering these features, ensuring that you are fully equipped to create stunning, professional-quality videos.

Keep in mind that practice and experimentation are the keys to mastering video editing. As you continue exploring CapCut, stay open to learning new techniques and refining your editing skills. The more you create, the more you will discover what works best for your projects, whether you're crafting social media content, educational videos, or creative short films.

Video editing is an evolving art, and with CapCut at your fingertips, the possibilities are endless. Let your creativity lead the way, and keep pushing the boundaries of what you can create. *[Your Honest review of this book will be much appreciated to help me fine-tune and advance the techniques employed in subsequent publications on this topic, so you can check back for updates on this guide. Thank you]*

GLOSSARY OF CAPCUT AND VIDEO EDITING TERMS

CapCut is a powerful tool for digital content creation, and understanding its features is essential to mastering video editing. This glossary provides an alphabetical list of key terms to help you navigate the editing process with ease.

- **Aspect Ratio**: The width-to-height ratio of your video frame, such as 16:9 for standard widescreen format.
- **Aspect Ratio Adjustment**: A tool that allows you to modify the aspect ratio to fit different platforms (e.g., 1:1 for Instagram, 9:16 for TikTok).
- **Audio Track**: A timeline layer dedicated to audio elements like music, sound effects, and voiceovers.

- **Blend Mode**: Settings that control how layers interact with each other, affecting their visibility and combination.
- **Blur Effect**: An effect that softens the focus of part of your video, often used for backgrounds or to de-emphasize specific areas.
- **Background Removal**: A feature that automatically detects and removes the background from video clips, allowing for easy compositing.
- **Canvas**: The background or base layer on which you arrange and position all other media elements in your project.
- **Chroma Key**: A technique that removes a specific color (often green) from a video to allow background replacement (green screen effect).
- **Clip**: A section of video or audio that can be edited and placed onto the timeline.

- **Color Grading**: Adjusting colors and tones to create a particular mood or aesthetic in your video.
- **Custom Stickers**: Personalized graphics or images created from videos or pictures that can be added to your project.
- **Crop**: A tool that allows you to cut out unwanted portions of a video or image clip, focusing on a specific area.
- **Effect**: Visual or audio modifications, such as blurs, distortions, or reverb, are used to enhance or change the appearance of clips.
- **Export**: The process of rendering and saving your edited video into a file format for sharing or viewing.
- **Filter**: Preset effects that alter the visual appearance of your video, such as adjusting colors or applying artistic styles.

- **Freeze Frame**: A technique that captures and holds a still image from a video clip for a set duration.
- **Keyframe**: A specific point in time where a value (e.g., position, opacity) is set, enabling animation by changing these values over time.
- **Layer**: Different levels of media, such as video, text, or images, are stacked on top of each other on the timeline.
- **Lip Sync**: Ensuring that the voiceover or audio matches the movements of the speaker's lips in a video.
- **LUT (Look-Up Table)**: A preset color grading profile that changes the look of your video to achieve a specific visual effect.
- **Masking**: A technique that hides or reveals specific parts of a clip using shapes or custom paths.

- **Mosaic Effect**: A pixelation effect applied to parts of a video to obscure details for privacy or stylistic reasons.
- **Mirror**: A visual effect that flips a video clip horizontally or vertically.
- **Overlay**: Media elements such as images, text, or videos that are placed on top of the main video track.
- **Overlay Modes**: Various blending options for overlays that define how they interact with the underlying media layers, such as Multiply or Screen.
- **Playback Controls**: Tools that allow you to play, pause, rewind, or fast forward through your project.
- **Playback Speed**: Adjusting the speed at which the video plays; speeding up can add excitement while slowing it down can emphasize key moments.

217

- **Presets**: Saved settings for effects, transitions, or color grading that can be quickly applied to multiple clips.
- **Project**: The working file in CapCut that stores all media, edits, and settings for your video.
- **Project File**: The file format used to save your CapCut project, contains all the video, audio, and editing information.
- **Preview Window**: The section where you can view your project as you edit it, making it easy to see changes in real-time.
- **Resolution**: The quality of the video, is defined by its dimensions in pixels (e.g., 1920x1080 for Full HD).
- **Reverse**: An effect that plays a clip backward, creating a unique visual impact.
- **Rotate** A tool that changes the orientation of a video clip by rotating it to different angles.

- **Split**: Dividing a single clip into multiple segments for further editing or to insert transitions.
- **Split Tool**: A feature that helps divide a clip into two or more segments.
- **Speed Curve**: A tool used to adjust playback speed in a nonlinear fashion, creating variable speed effects within a single clip.
- **Sticker**: Pre-designed graphics are added to your video, often for creative or decorative purposes.
- **Text-to-Speech**: A feature that converts written text into spoken audio, useful for voiceovers or narration.
- **Text Style**: Pre-designed templates for adding text with specific fonts, animations, and effects.
- **Timeline**: The area where you organize and arrange your media clips, audio tracks, and other elements in sequence.

- **Trim**: The process of removing unwanted sections from the start or end of a clip.
- **Trim Handles**: The points at the beginning and end of a clip that you can drag to trim its duration.
- **Transition**: Effects are used to create smooth changes from one clip to another, such as fades or dissolves.
- **Volume Envelope**: A tool that graphically represents the audio volume levels over time, allowing for precise control of fade-ins and fade-outs.
- **Voiceover**: A recording of spoken words added to the video to provide narration or commentary.
- **Waveform**: A visual representation of the audio's amplitude over time, helping you manage audio levels.

- **Zoom**: A tool that allows you to magnify or shrink the timeline view to help with detailed editing or getting an overview of the project.
- This glossary provides a comprehensive overview of the essential terms in CapCut and video editing, helping you navigate and enhance your creative process.

INDEX

U

user-friendly interface, 7, 9, 10, 65
using a desktop computer, 7

V

video, 1, 2, 3, 4, 5, 6, 7, 8, 9, 11, 12, 13,
    16, 21, 22, 23, 25, 26, 27, 28, 30, 31,
    32, 34, 35, 36, 37, 38, 40, 41, 42, 43,
    45, 55, 56, 57, 58, 59, 60, 61, 62, 64,
    65, 66, 67, 70, 71, 72, 73, 74, 75, 76,
    77, 78, 79, 82, 83, 85, 87, 88, 90, 91,
    94, 95, 96, 97,98, 99, 100, 101, 104,
    105, 106, 107, 108, 109, 110, 111,
    112, 115, 116, 117, 118, 121, 125,
    126, 127, 128, 129, 131, 132, 134,
    135, 136, 137, 138, 139, 140, 141,
    143, 144, 145, 146, 148, 149, 151,
    153, 154, 155, 156, 157, 158, 159,
    161, 162, 163, 164, 167, 169, 170,
    171, 179, 180, 181, 182, 183, 184,
    185, 186, 187, 188, 189, 190, 191,
    192, 193, 196, 197, 198, 199, 200,
    202, 203, 204, 205, 206, 208, 210,
    211, 213, 214, 215, 216, 217, 218,
    219, 220, 221
video aspect, 64
video editing application, 1, 5, 22, 157
video file, 73
Video Speed, 130
video-editing, 2
videos, 69
visual elements, 82, 88, 123, 153, 172
voice, 168
voiceovers, 38, 43, 166, 170, 175, 210,
    213, 219

W

window, 80

Z

zoom effect, 101, 115, 201, 202, 204
Zoom., 202
zooming in or out, 101